Speechwriting

A professional step-by-step guide for executives

Edward H. McCarthy

Speechwriting
A professional step-by-step guide for executives
By Edward H. McCarthy

Published by
The Executive Speaker® Company
Box 292437
Dayton, Ohio 45429

First Printing 1989
Printed in the United States of America
Library of Congress Catalog Card Number: 89-083450
ISBN: 0-930255-01-1

The table on page 15 is from *Speech: Dynamic Communication,* Second Edition, by Milton Dickens, copyright © by Harcourt Brace Jovanovich, Inc., and reprinted by permission of the publisher.

The quotation on pages 20 and 21 is from *Public Speaking: A Rhetorical Perspective,* Second Edition, by Jane Blankenship, copyright © 1972 by Jane Blankenship, and reprinted by permission of the author.

The quotation on page 60 is from *Printer's Ink* magazine, copyright © by Joseph Ecclesine and reprinted by permission of the author.

The quotation on pages 89 and 90 is from a speech titled "U.S. Competitiveness," by Fred G. Steingraber, copyright © 1987 by A. T. Kearney, Inc., and reprinted by permission of A. T. Kearney, Inc.

Cover design by Karen Alley.

Special discounts are available for bulk quantity orders by training organizations, corporations, schools and colleges, and others. Special printings or printings of excerpts are also available. For additional information write to:

Promotional Sales
The Executive Speaker® Company
Box 292437
Dayton, Ohio 45429

Acknowledgments

A special note of thanks is due Robert O. Skovgard, founder and publisher of *The Executive Speaker*® newsletter and *Executive Speeches*™ journal, for his help in editing and rewriting the early drafts, for his role in providing the quotations and examples used in this guide, and for his work in designing and formatting the book.

Thanks also to my wife, Carol, for her encouragement and proofreading of the final draft, and to Vivian Skovgard and Sue Hamby of *The Executive Speaker*® Company, for their editorial assistance.

I also owe a debt of thanks to Sid Cato for invaluable constructive criticism and assistance with publicity for the book.

E.H.M.

About the Author

Edward H. McCarthy is a government relations manager with the American Telephone and Telegraph Company in Chicago. He is also editor of *The Executive Speaker*® newsletter and a free-lance speechwriter and consultant. His experience includes 10 years in public relations during which time he served as president of the Publicity Club of Chicago. He is an award-winning annual report writer and newsletter editor. He earned graduate and undergraduate degrees in speech from Eastern Michigan University. A former educator, he has taught speech at the university and community college levels.

CONTENTS

PART I
PLANNING THE SPEECH

Topic • Statement of specific purpose • Thesis or central idea • Two to five main points that develop the thesis • Subpoints for each main point • Examples of how to structure a speech • 22 patterns for structuring a speech

PART II
WRITING THE SPEECH

Contents

INTRODUCTION

This book is designed for executives or managers who have little or no speechwriting experience and who are faced with the task of writing a speech for someone else—or themselves.

You may be a merchandising vice president, manufacturing manager, quality control director, systems engineer, lawyer, accountant or other professional. You have special expertise and you have a reputation for being articulate. But you lack specific knowledge of speechwriting principles and practices. This book gives you an easy to follow, step-by-step guide that will help you produce a competent, on-time, successful speech.

You may even be a professional writer in the communications or editorial services department—but you have never written a speech. Your experience and training is geared toward writing for the eye (printed materials) rather than writing for the ear (speeches). In that case, you will find in this book all the speechwriting tips and principles needed to get you quickly on your way while avoiding a lot of time-consuming wrong steps.

If you're a seasoned speechwriting professional, you should find this book a useful review and reinforcement of what you already know. It may be a welcome refresher.

The focus here is on speechwriting, not the entire speechmaking process. You won't be coached on delivery techniques. You won't be told how to merchandise the speech or what to do with hecklers in the audience or how to handle difficult questions during a question-and-answer session.

Those aspects were left out not because they are unimportant, but because the book's main focus is on what to do when you're asked to *write* a speech for someone else—or if you're writing one for yourself.

Although presentation techniques are important, it is the structure of the speech, the correct selection of supporting material, the phrasing, and the word selection that create the concepts and word pictures which impress themselves on the minds of the listeners. The most polished and glittering delivery can do little to rescue a poorly conceived and constructed speech. But a well-structured and well-written speech—even with a weak delivery—stands a good chance of being accepted by an audience.

The assumption here is that the speaker will be properly coached and will rehearse the speech several times. The speaker cannot leave the critical element of delivery to chance. As Chicago Bears head coach Mike Ditka said in his autobiography: "Anyone who thinks he can play without practicing is a fool." The same holds true for public speaking.

Overview

When you're first told you have to write the speech, avoid the "Oh no, what am I going to write?" trap. Don't even think about *writing* the speech at the outset.

Instead, focus your energies on the speech process presented in this book. It will keep you on track. It's your blueprint to success.

There are two stages in the process: planning and writing. Planning always comes first. Plan well and the actual writing of the speech will be easier.

Resist the temptation to start piling words on paper. You must first have a plan. Without such a plan, writing anything would be both meaningless and futile.

Part 1 of this book deals with planning and includes four main steps:

Step 1: Analysis of the audience and occasion;

Step 2: Initial meeting with the speaker to discuss the audience, select a topic, speech purpose, thesis, main points that will fully develop the thesis, and subpoints for the main points;

Step 3: Research for supporting material;

Step 4: Follow-up meeting with the speaker to discuss supporting material you have developed, and to reconfirm the speech purpose, thesis and outline of the speech body.

Part 2 of this book discusses writing the speech and also includes four main steps:

Step 1: Writing the speech body;

Step 2: Writing the introduction;

Step 3: Writing the conclusion;

Using transitions;

Using humor;

Step 4: Reviewing the draft with the speaker and writing the final version of the speech.

A note on time

An important aspect of planning and writing a speech is allocating your time. If you will be writing a typical 20-minute informative or persuasive speech, plan to spend at least 20-30 hours over a period of time. For obvious reasons, a speech of this kind cannot be completed in one or two long blocks of time. So plan to spend that 20-30 hours over several weeks.

As a general rule, a typical 20-minute speech will be broken down in the following way:

• Introduction: 2-3 minutes.

• Body: 14-16 minutes.

• Conclusion: 2-3 minutes.

One of the benefits of the systematic approach of this book is that it forces the writer to deal in bite-sized, manageable segments. Looking into the face of a two- to three-thousand-word speech is an imposing proposition.

But, looking at a two- or three-minute introduction, then the body section comprising several four- to six-minute segments, and then a closing of two- or three-minutes, is an entirely different and a far more doable thing.

Speechwriting is not easy. Properly done it is high adventure, it is very difficult, and it is highly satisfying. If you follow a plan and are guided by the suggestions in this book, you will increase the likelihood of a favorable outcome.

PART I

PLANNING
THE
SPEECH

STEP 1
Analyze the Audience and the Occasion

The first and most important step in writing the speech is to analyze your audience and study the occasion. Done well, it will pay huge dividends.

Every moment you spend in careful and original thinking about the audience will save you hours of time later. This information will serve as an infallible guide to decisions you will make later about every aspect of the speech. What kind of arguments will work best? The audience and occasion—or better, your analysis of the audience and occasion—will tell you. Which kinds of supporting material will be the most appropriate, most useful, most persuasive? Should you use humor? If so, where and what kind of humor?

How to best structure the speech? Your analysis of the audience and occasion will tell you.

Find out as much as you can about the demographics of the audience. That includes age, sex, religion, education, group membership, ethnic or cultural background, and other factors that provide specific, concrete information about the group.

Determine why the group is gathering and how many people will be in attendance. Is there a particular theme for the occasion? Will other speakers precede or follow the speaker you're writing for? If so, what are they speaking about? What does the group think about the occasion, the speaker, the speaker's company or organization? If a topic has already been selected for or by the speaker, what is the group's knowledge level of it? What is its attitude toward the topic? What is its interest level?

Even obvious, mechanical things, or seemingly meaningless details should be considered. In what city will the speech be presented? What hotel? What is the name of the banquet room? Can the the day, month, or year be related to the audience or topic? Outside elements like the weather, news items, politics, sports, movies, current best sellers, or books related to the audience's main interests can all be useful information. Gathering this kind of information is critically important because for the speech to be successful, the topic and all the supporting material used in it must be directly related to and adapted to the audience.

The audience is always the bottom line in the speech. It is the final arbiter. How well the material in the speech is adapted to and focused on the experiences, needs, and attitudes of the audience will determine, in large part, the speaker's effectiveness. If there is an anvil on which the metal of the speech is shaped and tested, it is the audience.

If a topic hasn't been selected, the speaker will have to choose one that can be directly related to the audience and is appropriate for the occasion. Even if the topic hasn't been selected at this point, the analysis of the audience and occasion can be done.

STEP 2
Meet with the Speaker to Develop the Outline

Meeting with the speaker is the first test of how well you have researched and analyzed the audience and how well you have examined the speech occasion. First, discuss in detail the information you've gleaned about the audience and occasion. Using that information, draw in the speaker's ideas and assumptions about the audience.

Select a topic if that hasn't already been done. Narrow the topic down because you can't cover everything about it in a typical 20-minute speech.

Use a tape recorder during the interview. Ask the speaker lots of questions and also take notes. Let the speaker do most of the talking. Restate ideas mentioned by the speaker and ask for details, or clarification, or amplification on what has been said. Be a good listener but don't be passive.

In his monthly *Executive Action* advisory, communication consultant James E. Lukaszewski featured a list of questions used by reporters when they are probing for information. These questions, or modifications of them, can be used to get the speaker to open up and expand on the subject:

Ask for clarification

- Exactly what do you mean?
- Say it again, please.
- What else?
- What do you mean by that word?

Ask for justification

- When you say that, what are you assuming?
- What's your reasoning on that?
- Is that all there's to it?
- What would someone on the other side say?

Refocus the question

- If that's so, what about...?
- How would you relate that to this...?
- How does [someone's] statement relate to...?
- Let's take a closer look at that.

Prompt the speaker

- If you say that, then you mean this. Right?
- Here's one answer to that...

Redirect the question

- Do you agree?
- How would you answer that?[1]

Pay particular attention to the speaker's thought process and speaking style. Also closely monitor those ideas the speaker seems to like best and least. Look for favorite phrases the speaker uses. Try to draw out a few personal anecdotes. Pay attention to names and resources the speaker mentions on where to get some of the information you will need.

Note what, if any, sense of humor the speaker has. Do one-liners or humorous insights come up naturally? Is the speaker a storyteller? In the same vein, does the speaker naturally turn to figures of speech, or frequently quote a favorite author?

During the initial session, you and the speaker should develop an outline of the speech body. The outline should include:

- A statement of the specific purpose of the speech (what the speaker hopes to accomplish),
- A thesis (also called central idea or core statement), and
- Two to five main points that develop different aspects of the thesis.

The thesis will give unity to the speech. Just as everything in the speech should have some relevance to the audience, it should also have something to do with the thesis.

The thesis can be either stated or implied. Think of the thesis this way: If the topic is what the speaker is speaking about, the thesis is either what the speaker thinks about the topic or is the speaker's point of view on the topic. For example, the subject of this book is speechwriting. The thesis or author's point of view on the subject is that if you develop a good plan and follow the basic steps and rules in this book, you will increase your chances of writing a successful speech.

Develop subpoints for each main point. Subpoints are the principal divisions of main points. Although this is a mechanical and elemental point, do not place supporting material directly under one of the main points. Supporting material should be organized under the subpoints.

Structure the main points in a meaningful and consistent pattern. Three of the more common organizational patterns are **topical** ("The two main aspects of speechwriting are planning and writing."), **spatial** ("We'll review objectives and results on a region by region basis.") and **time** ("We'll look at the past performance, present status, and future outlook for the Midwest Division.").

There's no limit to the different patterns you can develop. It must first meet the requirements and needs of the audience and second, must form a meaningful relationship and be internally consistent. In total, the main points should fully develop the speaker's thesis.

Here's a coherent pattern of main points from a speech titled "Communication and Credibility: Corporate Speechmaking in an Incredulous Age," [2] by Jerry Tarver, author of *Professional Speech Writing*. Members of the International Association of Business Communicators were his audience. Note that a topical pattern is used. This pattern is perhaps the most flexible and requires the speaker to have a high degree of expertise in the subject.

Thesis

I submit that corporate speechmaking is an indispensable weapon in the communications arsenal you must maintain to gain credibility in our incredulous age.

Body

I. (Main Point)	Why speech is a credible medium
A. (Subpoint)	Speech humanizes your message
B. (Subpoint)	Speech is readily adaptable to an audience's needs and interests
C. (Subpoint)	Speech permits interaction
D. (Subpoint)	Speechmaking allows you to probe an issue in considerable depth
II. (Main Point)	Major problems in running a speaking program
A. (Subpoint)	Lack of purpose
B. (Subpoint)	Failing to measure results
C. (Subpoint)	Poor speakers
D. (Subpoint)	Lack of status and staff to do the job

11

Given the nature and needs of the audience (communication professionals) and the background of the speaker as an expert on speech, the use of the topical pattern was appropriate. It allowed an open format for the speaker to make his point about an area of interest to members of the audience and then to focus attention on problem areas of interest to them.

Here's another example of a solid, consistent structure of main points from a speech by speechwriter and communications consultant, John Bonée. It, too, is a topical pattern. His remarks, titled "The Care and Feeding of The Executive Speaker: A Few Age Old Principles of Effective Oratory,"[3] were delivered at the National Conference of the Public Relations Students Society of America.

Thesis

The speaker's thesis is that there are two kinds of problems or barriers to writing a successful speech for an executive. One is theoretical and the other is practical.

Preview of Body

In the first part, I'm going to talk about the theoretical barriers to successful speech writing and to the successful management, if you will, of the speaker. Barriers that are rather intellectual than practical. In the second part I'll talk about some practical problems you meet in dealing with your client.

Body

I. (Main Point)   Theoretical problems to successful speech writing

A. (Subpoint)	The speaker's prejudice in favor of logic over rhetoric, of sweet reason over emotional appeal— a prejudice in favor of the facts, the data, the information over any other kind of argumentation
B. (Subpoint)	The speaker's insistence on saying everything instead of limiting the message
C. (Subpoint)	The speaker's prejudice in favor of visual aids
D. (Subpoint)	The speaker's prejudice in favor of a written style
II. (Main Point)	Practical problems to successful speech writing
A. (Subpoint)	Speaker-writer interface
B. (Subpoint)	Clearances of manuscript
C. (Subpoint)	Merchandising the speech

The next example of an effective structure of main points uses the time pattern. The occasion is a Harvard Business School alumni luncheon and the speaker, Allen Born, of AMAX, Inc., discusses what had to be done to turn his company around. The audience and occasion required a straightforward and quick-paced narrative—ideally suited to the chronological structure. The speech was titled "800 Days: Trauma, Decision, Action."[4]

Introduction

. . . When you first walk in the door of a troubled company, you ask yourself, "Have I made the right decision? Do I really need this again?" Then as the situations unfold, you find the early days are a nightmare. To do the job on a patient who's been labeled "terminal" requires many talents. You have to be a surgeon, chef, and orchestra conductor.

Body

I. (Main Point)	The first 100 days: Trauma and Decision
II. (Main Point)	The next 200 days: Decision and Action
III. (Main Point)	The next 400 days: Action, Strategy and Opportunity
IV. (Main Point)	The next 100 days: Continued Action and Opportunity

Conclusion

Which brings us to today. The 800 days are history. What have we accomplished since June 1985? We've saved a dying patient, breathed new life into him and created a new AMAX, a company capable of surviving and prospering in the competitive world of energy, minerals and manufacturing.

Notice how each of the examples used above allows the speaker to develop his own point of view while smoothly moving the speech forward. At the same time, each one of the structures can be kept clearly in mind by the listeners and aids them in following the speech. A number of specific devices and techniques for gaining and keeping attention will be presented in Part II of this book, but you should be aware that a carefully ordered and coherent structure is the most basic means a speaker has to maintain audience attention and interest.

To trigger a multitude of ways to structure the main points of the body of the speech, here are

22 time-tested patterns from author Milton Dickens' second edition of *Speech: Dynamic Communication*. These, and variations of them, have been used extensively with much success. The pattern you choose must be consistent and must fully develop the thesis.

1. Past, present, future (or other time sequence)
2. Local, state, national, international (or other space sequence)
3. Cause, effect
4. Need, desirability, practicality, alternatives
5. Problem-solution
6. Who, what, why, when, how, where
7. Advantages, disadvantages
8. Attention, need, satisfaction, visualization, action
9. Theory, practice
10. Physical, mental, emotional, spiritual
11. Heredity, environment
12. Thinking, feeling, doing
13. Structure, function
14. Political, economic, social
15. Resemblances, differences
16. Background, characteristics, accomplishments
17. Stop, look, listen
18. Symptoms, prevention, cure
19. Extended analogy
20. Partitioning a quotation
21. ABC's (or other letter combination)
22. Spelling a key word[5]

The areas just covered—**topic, specific purpose, thesis, main points, subpoints**—are the minimum you and the speaker should take away from your first meeting. Both of you should be in full agreement on these important basics.

Ideally, you also will have drawn information from the speaker—an anecdote that can be used in illustrating a point, the speaker's suggestions on statistics, or insights on sources of information that can be used in the speech. Beyond that you should take away a wealth of your own insights on the speaker's way of thinking and speaking.

At this point, you have analyzed the audience and occasion and have completed your first meeting with the speaker. You should have an outline of the main points and subpoints in hand so you know exactly where you're going and how. Think of it as your roadmap to success.

Outlining is a proven, effective way to organize thoughts. A thoughtful and well-prepared speech outline will keep the speaker on track. It will enable the listeners to easily follow and remember what the speaker says. As a result, it will maximize the speaker's chances of achieving a desired result or specific purpose.

REVIEW

Planning the Speech

I. Analyze the audience and occasion

II. Meet with the speaker to develop outline
   A. Discuss audience analysis
   B. Discuss topic and speech purpose
   C. Develop thesis
   D. Develop main points
   E. Develop subpoints

STEP 3
Do Research for Supporting Material

Now it's time to gather supporting material—proof, details, evidence—for the sub-points under each main point. Think of this step as gathering meat to put on the bones of the skeleton—the outline that you and the speaker developed. Generally, supporting material includes examples, statistics, anecdotes, testimony and analogies. Sometimes, of course, supporting material will be a combination of two or more kinds.

You should gather at least three or four times as much information as you'll need to support each subpoint. Vary the kinds of supporting materials you select for each one. Your speechwriting task later will be made much easier if you can select the most appropriate supports for a particular subpoint from many choices. If you have limited yourself, you could find out that something you thought was a sure-fire support just isn't going to work. Now is the time to eliminate that from happening.

As you conduct your research, you'll undoubtedly find yourself quickly and easily weeding out extraneous and inappropriate material. That's because of the audience analysis you did as well as the *thesis-main point-subpoint* groundwork you and the speaker laid.

Don't rely too heavily on one kind of supporting material. Balance is what you should seek. Your knowledge of the audience will play a major role in which kinds and how much supporting material to use.

To test the effectiveness of any supporting material, use this short series of questions developed by Jane Blankenship in *Public Speaking: A Rhetorical Perspective:*

1. Is my material relevant to my speech?
2. Is my material accurate? Does it come from a reliable source?
3. Is my material recent enough?
4. Is my material fairly stated? Are my examples typical? Is my information sufficient in scope to present an accurate picture?
5. Is my material appropriate to this particular audience? Will it be meaningful to them?
6. Is my material interesting and vivid?

If the supporting material meets the first five requirements, it will be acceptable as rhetorical proof. If it also meets the sixth, it will have still a better chance of being accepted by your audience.[6]

Once you've gathered and tested the supporting material, rough in several possibilities under each subpoint below your main points. Also rough in those supporting materials the speaker mentioned during your first meeting that would be appropriate for the topic, audience, and occasion. If they meet the tests of appropriateness, the speaker has the right to see them. Remember, the supporting materials should be audience centered.

Leave the visual aids at home for most executive speeches. They are more appropriate for use in sales or instructional presentations, boardroom reports and the like than for typical public speaking situations.

Below are selections of supporting material from speeches by executives. They were chosen from the extensive library of executive speeches maintained by *The Executive Speaker*® Company because they met the tests of supporting material in the speeches in which they were used. They also illustrate the various types of supporting material.

Examples

Examples are a specific part or aspect of a subject. They are strong point-making sources because it is easier for the listener to grasp and understand a specific part or aspect of a subject than to try to comprehend a more general or abstract version of it. For example, if your speaker is talking about brand names, listeners will grasp the point more quickly if you mention *Ivory* soap or *Coca-Cola*. Dealing in specific, concrete, easily-grasped images, applies to all areas of speechwriting.

Examples can be hypothetical or factual and are either detailed or undetailed. Sometimes, several undetailed examples can effectively make a point. At other times, a single detailed example that amplifies, explains or illustrates a point is the most effective.

Undetailed Examples

Undetailed examples can be as brief as one sentence. They can be longer, of course, but are lighter on details.

1 The most important thing we need to know about communicating is that much of what we assume we know about it is wrong. The fact is that we've done a miserable job of communicating about communications.

Undetailed Examples

Babies start communicating when they give that first wail after birth. By the time they're three they're pretty good at making their wishes and objections known. So we've let the impression develop that communicating is simple—it's child's play; everyone learns to do it naturally, like walking. And even though the massive troubles that beset our age reflect breakdowns in communication—wars, crime, divorce, social upheavals—we're giving less and less attention in schools to making sure that children learn at least the fundamental skills needed to communicate.[7]

2 Customers and investors are smarter and more sophisticated than ever before. You can't

fool them for very long. The consumer and investor both want good value at a fair price.

The classic example is automobiles. The U.S. industry kept on making the cars the way they wanted to make them long after customers began sending them signals. The customer wanted better quality. The customer wanted better efficiency. The Japanese came along and provided what they wanted. Now Japanese cars, which were scorned in the 1960s, are known for their quality and their value.[8]

3 We simply can't live without risks. We can study them. We can, and we must minimize them. But we'll never eliminate them completely.

Undetailed Examples

As a recent example, one of only three producers of whooping cough vaccine, Connaught Laboratories, recently announced that it was getting out of the market. They can't afford the liability insurance any longer.

Parents of children who have suffered very rare, but serious side effects have won multi-million dollar lawsuits. That has forced the cost of insurance to where it's no longer profitable for some companies to make the drug. Whooping cough once killed 7,000 American children a year and infected a quarter million more.

How many die from the vaccine? On average, less than 10 a year. It's easy usually to find solutions to problems—if you ignore the problems created by those solutions.[9]

4 I believe journalists do a far better job of covering business than we have a right to expect. In the oil industry, we don't send a chemist out to do a geologist's job. Yet too often we expect journalists to know everything about every part

23

of our business. That's a double standard. And a crying shame.

Truth is, the simple ratio of businesses to news media does not allow the news media to specialize the way businesses do. And business should recognize this fact.

Here in Gainesville there are more than 2,000 businesses. Compare these 2,000 businesses with two television stations, two daily newspapers, six radio stations and a handful of magazines and weeklies. It doesn't take a genius to figure out that journalists are sadly outnumbered. Custer had better odds at Little Big Horn.

Even so, that does not excuse journalists who cover business from their responsibility to be fair and accurate. But it does place a burden on both business people and journalists to get along, to cooperate and help each other communicate with the public.[10]

Undetailed Examples

5 In a capitalistic society, money is an index of social worth. Children today see that the big money goes not to the brainiest, the most literate, or the most dedicated humanitarians, but to the so-called "superstars"—a misnomer if ever I heard one, since many display questionable talent, underexercised intellects, and somewhat weird public behavior. Their social contributions consist primarily in momentary entertainment for their fans. With the big money they receive, however, go special privileges, amnesty for outrageous social and legal transgressions, and incredible power.

I understand that an Astro fan is asking Houstonians to send in $7.00 each to make up the difference between the quarter million dollars a player is demanding and the $180,000 the Astros are willing to pay him. When is the last time you heard of anyone collecting money to supplement a teacher's minimum wage? Does this suggest our priorities may be awry?[11]

Detailed Examples

1 At the top of my speech, I told you a story about shoes. I'd like to close with another shoe story. It's a story that I think you folks in the inventory control field will appreciate. The only thing that keeps this story from being totally satisfying to an American audience concerned about quality in American-made products is that the shoe itself is constructed overseas. Nevertheless, it was an American-conceived idea, and everything but the manufacturing process is handled in the United States.

Jeffrey N. Silverman is only 27-years-old, but his company—Toddler University—produces a quality shoe that yuppie parents pay $40 a pair to put their children's feet in. The shoes look like a jogging shoe that has been scaled down for tiny feet. They are well styled. And unlike many children's shoes, the soles are stitched on rather than glued. A quality product.

Silverman owes much of his success to figuring out how to control inventory. And it just so happens that his inventory secret has a side benefit for parents. Normally children's shoes are produced in 11 different sizes, each with five widths. Shoe stores find it difficult to keep so many children's shoes in so many sizes and widths. Their stock rooms can't hold them all, and if they are out of one size and width, it takes weeks to restock. This frustrates parents, who often must go from store to store before they can find a shoe that fits.

Silverman's solution is elegantly simple. He produces 11 sizes but only one width. Inserts

Detailed Examples

that are easily removed change the width on each shoe. This means that parents can easily change the width of their children's shoes without having to buy a new pair. Silverman has figured out how to give his customers what they want, and he gets it to them when they want it. He has a quality operation.[12]

2 Some of our most useful products, like vaccines and an anti-nausea drug we had for expectant women, have been discontinued. Why have they been discontinued? I think the prime example is the drug, Benedectin, which was made by Merrell.

Detailed Examples

We bought the Merrell Pharmaceutical Division from Richardson-Merrell a number of years ago and created Merrell-Dow Pharmaceuticals. Well, they had this drug which had been given to thirty-three million women around the world. Proven safe throughout the decades. The FDA in the U.S., the equivalent to FDA in Great Britain—everybody—after testing and retesting said, "The drug is completely safe!" But three percent of all children are born with some defect, whether you give the mother anything or nothing. Now, three percent of thirty-three million is about one million potentially defective children. And some smart lawyer invented taking a few hundred of those and bringing suit on this drug.

Why did we discontinue it? At one point, our sales in the United States were 20 million dollars a year. Our legal and insurance costs reached 18 million dollars; so our sales and our costs were the same. Now you also have the cost of producing and marketing the product. It was losing so much money that we felt we had to discontinue it. We had 12,000 doctors in this country who said, "Please don't do this. This is a useful drug." But we just could not bear that any more.

But, those aren't the only costs. Our management, including myself, spend more time being deposed, appearing in court, and so forth, than you can possibly imagine. I wasted more than 20 working days in 1986 alone on legal cases. And that's part of the game the lawyers are playing right now. You know, that's almost 10 percent of my total time.

We have a case that I'm being deposed this month of February. It's not against us, it's against some other company but, since we were involved as a customer of theirs, they figure that if they go and try to tie me up, I won't do it because it's for some other company and they'll eventually get a settlement from the other company. I'm fooling them—I'm going to appear. But it means four hours of deposition, probably about four hours of preparation for that and there is one working day essentially shot for a deposition that doesn't even involve a suit against The Dow Chemical Company, but against a company that sold us something!

Detailed Examples

So this is one of the most powerful weapons the trial lawyers have, using up executive time, and the time of the whole organization.[13]

3 Everybody loves a bargain. In the United States and many other countries, we offer "free gifts" just for trying a product. They cost the public nothing. In fact, we can prove that a free offer actually reduces the cost of a product because it induces more people to try the product. Many of those who try, will buy. The higher the volume, the lower the cost. Sounds like a very constructive business practice, right? Wrong. At least it's wrong in Norway. There, the

government has banned the use of the word "free" from all sales literature, arguing that nothing is free, that the cost of the premium is ultimately reflected in the cost of the product.

We cannot even send the customer a "free sample" of the book or magazine we are trying to sell him! Result: everyone loses. We lose the chance to introduce potential customers to our products. Customers lose the chance to get something for nothing. And, in fact, our sales in Norway dropped by half when that rule took effect. Norway—and other countries too—protects its consumers—whether the consumers like it or not! And who loses as a result of this protection? The consumer!

Detailed Examples

Sometimes, even if government changes its mind and consumers cheer the change, you still have to convince your own colleagues in order to gain local acceptance. The Norwegian government recently proposed to lift the ban on free gifts. Norway's consumer association thoroughly approved. But now industry is lining up to oppose giving premiums. In effect they're saying, "Let's save money by not giving anything away." My point here is that even though government and the consumer association have agreed that premiums can be beneficial, our Norwegian managers now must persuade their own colleagues in direct marketing that this is the case. Working through local trade associations, we are attempting to do just that—to convince our Norwegian friends that premiums are simply another effective form of advertising.[14]

Hypothetical Examples

Examples of this kind can be hard to create. That's because it is often difficult to make hypothetical examples plausible and realistic. They do, nevertheless, have an important role in your arsenal of supporting material.

1 Let me start by taking you 10 years or so into the future—a deregulated future for the electric power industry. We have met here in Atlanta to assess the results of sweeping deregulation.

And we've met in this hotel, which decided— some years ago—to cut the wires that bound it to Georgia Power Company. The hotel's owners made that decision when they were approached—by one of those enterprising, new, independent power producers that sprang up in the wake of deregulation. These folks offered the hotel a supply of bargain-priced electricity.

[The Room Lights Go Out]

What happened? Maybe the independent power producer took on too many bargain-seeking customers—and the peak demand on this hot afternoon exceeded its capacity. Or—with demand greater than supply—did another customer offer to pay a higher price than the hotel agreed to pay? Or did the independent power producer shave its estimate of needed reserves, to cut costs so it could offer lower prices?

[Lights On]

Well, of course, we could have tailored the nation's new, competitive energy policy to prevent disasters like that. We could have built into the policy a set of laws and regulations that governed reserve levels for independent power producers. And we could have made rules that covered the terms of electricity-supply contracts

Hypothetical Examples

between them and their customers. Then, we could have set up regulatory bodies to enforce those laws, regulations, and rules. But that wouldn't really be deregulation—would it?

Let's look at another scenario. Same people gathered in a meeting. Same place—this hotel in Atlanta. Same time—10 years down the road, into the age of deregulation.

This time the hotel owners have followed a different course. They brought in a renowned energy consultant, and he mapped out a wonderful plan for them. They need hot water— for the kitchens, the laundry, and the guest rooms. They also need electricity. Therefore— the expert tells them—the smart thing is to cogenerate.

Hypothetical Examples

He designs a neat system that produces steam. The steam drives a turbine, generating electricity. That same steam—which still has a lot of heat in it—then runs through heat-exchangers where it is condensed and, at the same time, transfers much of its heat to water. This heated water takes care of the kitchens, the laundry, and the guest rooms.

It takes some capital to set the system up. And some operating expense to keep it going. And some fuel expense to make the heat.

But, heck—they're paying to have tons of garbage hauled away every day. They can burn that for at least part of the fuel.

And if they make more electricity than the hotel needs, they may even be able to sell the excess to the power company. Isn't there some law that lets them do that—PURPA [Public Utilities Regulatory Policies Act], or something funny-sounding like that?

[Lights Out]

The system broke down. The energy consultant didn't tell them that burning garbage isn't quite the foolproof and trouble-free technology that some people think it is. The hotel manager got on the telephone to Georgia Power quick. But Georgia Power said, "Sorry—remember when you decided not to pay us a standby fee for agreeing to supply backup power? Ya'll have a nice day."[15]

2 It can be discouraging to realize, as one considers embarking on a new nuclear project, that perhaps there is a grammar school student somewhere who may grow up...develop acne and recover from it...have his teeth straightened...graduate from college...go to law school...pass the bar...and be able to stop your project in its tracks the day before it's supposed to come on-line.[16]

Hypothetical Examples

3 Within the data communications industry, the migration to new digital technologies is moving forward through a series of tests now under way.

Foremost are the ISDN [Integrated Services Digital Network] trials. ISDN is now in a test of new equipment, software and procedures to transmit voice, data and images simultaneously over existing telephone lines. The results of the ISDN trials could give Americans a door to future productivity and convenience.

Here's an idea of how it could affect our daily lives: The voice/data terminal in your office alerts you that the scheduled appointment with a key customer has been moved up a day.

Your broker's call from her car phone will include a video display of stock listings. You decide to purchase additional shares of a stock and reallocate funds from your money market account. The instant transaction yields you a 12-hundred dollar profit...take the rest of the day off.

At home, your daughter and her classmate across town are comparing a geography assignment, each drawing lines on a map from their home terminals.

Hypothetical Examples

And your son's efforts to do research from an on-line database service is traveling the same connections.

All of these messages...voice, data and video...will use the same public telecommunications system.[17]

Statistics

Statistics are necessary and useful when making a specific point. But they should be used sparingly. Don't bore the audience with dry, endless statistics. Instead, use only those that are relevant and meaningful. Try to present them as uniquely as you possibly can. Bring them to life. After all, they aren't just numbers. There are people, places, things, and events behind them.

Statistics

Remember that statistics measure things and the way measurements are brought into comprehension is through comparing the item being measured with a known quantity or familiar item. Just as a primitive man could better comprehend the meaning of a long distance by comparing it with 100—or 1,000—segments, each as long as his foot, so too, should any statistic you use in a speech be related to something with which a listener is familiar.

1 Recruiting, hiring, training, compensation and motivation, now all become the key to the code of successful competition in our industry of the future. Hiring the best people in the industry, while a substantial first step, is not enough; we must train them—and our industry has had an abysmal record of training its people—and we must compensate them to perform and behave in a manner which delivers the best customer service possible to our customers.

When you visit McDonald's you know, if the person who takes your order is taking his or her very first order for a McDonald's hamburger, he has had eighty hours of training. Eighty hours— for a $2.00 hamburger.[18]

2 When I started with the Royal Bank in 1939, we still kept ledgers by hand, with a straight pen—the kind you dip in an inkwell. We were a big corporation even then—world assets of 960 million dollars and 7,000 employees.

Statistics

Today, we have assets of 87 billion dollars and 40 thousand employees. But without modern technology—if we still did things the way we did 46 years ago—we'd need 600,000 men and women on our staff.

Except of course that we wouldn't be in business because we couldn't compete. . . .[19]

3 So when you hear the next prophecy about the fall of the newspaper business, you might stop and ask yourself the following question: What carries 30 million bits of storable information, weighs less than three pounds, provides hard copy, handles both text and graphics, allows random access, is available 24 hours a day, is completely portable and costs less than

30 cents a connect-hour (because it is paid for mostly by someone other than the customer)?

It is not the latest piece of fancy computer hardware. It is, as you know, the daily newspaper. Perhaps that's why every day 107 million Americans—seven out of ten adults—read one or more daily newspapers.[20]

Statistics

4 Twenty years ago, the entire Asian economy was half the size of Europe's and one-third that of the United States'. Today, the ratio is 75 percent in both cases—and the gap is closing fast, as the Pacific has replaced the western alliance—the U.K. and Europe—as the United States' principal trading partner.

It is always an eye-opener to learn that 60 percent of all the world's teenagers are now living on the Pacific Rim. So, human resources abound. . . .[21]

Anecdotes

Anecdotes can enliven any speech. They generally stem from a speaker's background, experience and expertise. They boost the speaker's credibility and believability. While anecdotes about respected or famous people can be effective, the most successful ones in speeches are usually personal.

Anecdotes

1 An American consultant we know lectures on project management at the Dailen Management School in China. He was asked to visit a group of Chinese businessmen in a nearby port city to explain, "How do you compute profit?" Our American friend was met at the railroad station by the Chinese spokesman for the group who said, "Please forgive me—I told you we would

meet with about 30 individuals to hear you explain about profit. But I must apologize—you will have an audience of more than 200. I hope you won't mind!" [22]

2 Forty years ago, when I sat where you do today, I received some simple advice that has stayed with me from a family friend named Marion Folsom, the architect of our nation's social security system and then a top executive of the Eastman Kodak Company.

"Bill," Mr. Folsom said, "you're going to find that 95 percent of all the decisions you'll ever make in your career could be made as well, by any reasonably intelligent high school sophomore. But they'll pay you for the other five percent."

And it's those five percent ladies and gentlemen that will be the most difficult—the kind of subjective 51-49 decisions that will call into play your own long-term vision...your corporate ideals...the discipline and constancy of your character.

Anecdotes

If, in making these decisions you rely on clear ethical principles...a firm commitment toward ethical behavior...and an inflexible standard of what's right and what's wrong...then your track record will be very good indeed.

Moreover, if you use such personal standards to set corporate standards—you will exemplify the kind of business leader that seems in such short supply today. [23]

3 Back in the mid-1950s at the hospital where I practiced, there was an elderly Czecho-slovakian gentleman admitted with a cancer of the windpipe, having a great deal of difficulty

Anecdotes

breathing and speaking. I was explaining to the interns, residents and medical students—probably talking in some very clinical terms—the signs that this man evidenced that should lead them to the diagnosis without any long and extensive evaluation or studies. The man reached up and tugged my sleeve until he had my head down near him where he could whisper in my ear and said, "Doctor, please remember there is a man inside." That's what it is all about.[24]

Testimony

Testimony is a quotation or paraphrase from a highly credible or authoritative source. Quotations from non-authoritative sources are also useful as long as they help the speaker to develop a point or round out an idea. However, they should be used sparingly, not simply to fill time.

Testimony

1 In the end, as we look at the value of technology in the practice of public relations, we should be preoccupied with the age-old question of how it will help us to communicate better, not whether we should buy it because some salesperson or colleague says we should. It is in communication, after all, that we succeed or fail in our mission as practitioners. At the same time, we must frame our answers in the context of what the best communication is all about.

As the great journalist Edward R. Murrow advised us: "Communication systems are neutral. They have neither conscience nor morality. . . . They will broadcast truth or falsehood and, I might add, quality or junk, with equal facility. Man communicating with man presents not the

problem of how to say it but, more fundamen-
tally, what he is to say" [25]

2 According to Peter Drucker, Professor of
Social Sciences at the Claremont Graduate
School in California, high tech will continue to
be tremendously important to our nation's
development in the future. But he says that new
job creation is mostly in low-tech businesses.
According to Drucker, 80 of the 100 companies
growing most rapidly recently have been
decidedly low technology—things like women's
wear manufacturers, restaurant chains, and
others. Drucker attributes the biggest reason for
the explosion of low-tech business to "a body of
organized knowledge of entrepreneurship and
innovation" in America—a managerial
breakthrough.[26]

Testimony

3 There is an old cliche that says, "It takes so
little to be above average." As women managers
we must learn that as we branch out we must
continue to produce a quality performance. Bear
Bryant, the legendary Alabama football coach,
was once asked to explain his successful record.
His response was, "It is the itsy-bitsy teeny-
weeny things that beat you."

For women managers, that lesson must become second nature to us. Quality and professional advancement are dependent upon
successfully handling the itsy-bitsy teeny-weeny
things. Each of us has to study our present
situation to discover the available opportunities
for honing our skills and propelling us forward
professionally.[27]

4 I'll close with a quote from former U.S. Commissioner of Education and author John Gardner. Every college's philosophy and practices should embrace John Gardner's thesis. He said, "An excellent plumber is infinitely more admirable than an incompetent philosopher. The society which scorns excellence in plumbing because plumbing is a humble activity and tolerates shoddiness in philosophy because it is an exalted activity will have neither good plumbing nor good philosophy. Neither its pipes nor its theories will hold water."

Whatever the training or retraining requirements in our area, we need to keep "the plumber's philosophy" in mind. Community colleges are just now beginning to be recognized for our contributions to advancing technology, economic development and the strengthening of our nation's position in the world market. Our standards of excellence and our responsiveness to the local employment market are building that reputation.[28]

Testimony

5 W. Edwards Deming's emphasis is that each company should hire a competent statistician and get on with the business of making improvements. He emphasizes that corporate management in America has five deadly diseases and unless they begin a transformation in management style, they will not be able to reverse the conditions that currently inhibit productivity and erode the ability of these companies to compete in the global marketplace. . . .

The five deadly diseases are: Lack of constancy of purpose symptomized by short-term thinking; emphasis on short-term profit; annual rating of performance of salaried employees, MBO [Management By Objectives] that nourishes

short-term performance; mobility of management caused by annual ratings that encourage
changing companies in search of higher wages;
and management's use of visible figures only
disregarding unknowns and unknowables, such
as the multiplying effect of a happy customer.[29]

Analogies

Used properly, figurative and literal analogies
can be vivid and compelling as supporting
material. Literal analogies look at things that are
basically in the same class or category and compare them. Figurative analogies look at things
that are in a different class or category and
compare them. Figurative analogies are said to be
more useful in illustrating a point than in proving
one, while literal analogies are best for proving
points. However, both can enhance meaning or
clarity and make a point quite effectively.

1 Lobbying is I suppose, much like mountain
climbing. You gather your teams, look at the
mountain from every possible perspective, study
the experiences of those who have been there
before you, develop your strategy, check your
equipment and begin the climb. With your goal
as your compass, you overcome the differing
view of the horizon with every turn. The higher
you advance, the colder and more hostile the
environment becomes. Sometimes, it's very
lonely, quiet, almost peaceful, but soon the
winds pick up, storm clouds appear and suddenly the screeching of those seeking to
preserve the status quo, confront your every
effort to achieve your goal. It's never easy—there
are no simple trails to follow—you make your
own. But you persevere, knowing you're on the

Analogies

right course. Seldom do you go straight from ground zero to the pinnacle. You usually take one peak at a time—a sub-committee, a full committee—the floor of the House of Representatives, then you repeat the process in the Senate, then perhaps a conference committee—and sometimes into the White House urging either a veto or a signature—sometimes you're forced into a crevice because it's the only way you can get from point A to point B. Setbacks always confront you, unexpected storms come up out of nowhere but you don't let them intimidate you, you do what you must do to survive, so that you can live to fight again. And fight you will—the wheels of democracy grind ever so slowly, but grind on they do. It's a tough, protracted and grueling process.[30]

Analogies

2 In other words, while depressed economic conditions may have been the complications to which the bank succumbed, the disease of managerial weakness debilitated it and made it susceptible to those complications.

Though analogies alone don't prove anything, one analogy suggests itself to me here. I collect antique Indian pottery. Dealers will sometimes take cracked and broken pottery and glue it back together so skillfully that the flaws don't show. One test to see if a piece has been repaired that way is to plunge it into a bucket of cold water. If it has been cracked, the crack will reappear. If it has been broken, it is likely to fall apart. For a bank, a depressed economic environment is like a bucket of cold water.[31]

3 We think sending people to one company for loans, another for insurance, and a third for brokerage services makes about as much sense

as sending them to one store for eggs, a second for meat, and a third for bread.[32]

4 It's pretty hard to play offense, to put some points on the board, if you don't have the ball. And the guys in the grandstand have made it pretty hard for us to get our hands on the ball. Because we don't compete in a vacuum; we compete within the framework of the U.S. economy and the rules and policies that affect it.[33]

5 At first glance, there doesn't appear to be much in common between your industry and mine. Except, of course, that our stores and support facilities couldn't operate without the electricity you generate.

Analogies

The differences between us are easier to identify: your companies are capital-intensive. Mine is labor-intensive and inventory-intensive. You are essentially manufacturers and marketers of a fundamental commodity. While we in retail buy and re-sell merchandise that appeals to diverse tastes and lifestyles.

Most dramatic of all is that the vast majority of your companies are government-regulated. While retailers are regulated by the competitive marketplace. Our success is determined not by rate levels, but by value competitiveness and an ability to respond to market conditions better and quicker than the merchant down the street.

Given these contrasts, I cannot hope to understand as well as you the problems and opportunities being faced by the electric utility industry today. So I won't be offering you unneeded advice on how to address them.

But, after 40 years in retailing, I do understand the demands of the competitive marketplace. And the strategies one needs to employ to be successful in it. That's what I will be discussing today. . . .[34]

Combinations of Supporting Material

Example

*Hypothetical
Quotation*

Quotation

1 Perhaps this shift in American values was best captured by Canadian writer Henry Makow.

Several years ago, he introduced a new board game called, *A Question of Scruples.* The game caught on, in part, because it addresses moral dilemmas you and I face every day, but usually don't talk about.

The players ask themselves tough ethical questions, like:

"Your car will soon need a new transmission. Do you sell it without telling the buyer?" Different players give different answers. And the winner is *not* the one who answers best, but the one who best anticipates the answers of others.

It strikes me tonight that this game—which seems to suggest that nothing is really wrong anymore—so aptly represents the ethical standards of the 1980s—a decade some have called the "decade of moral anarchy. . . ."

. . . Many of you recall the great defense tackle, Big Daddy Lipscomb, who starred in the National Football League.

He once described his tackling technique this way. He said: "I just wrap my arms around the whole backfield and peel 'em off one by one until I get to the ball carrier. Him...I keep."

Big Daddy's tackling method made him the terror of the turf. And maybe this same method can help us better grasp what ethics really is. So let's grab the whole backfield of 1980s views about ethics...peel off the wrong views one by one—and when we find the right view, let's keep it. . . .

. . . Paul Sand is an executive director of the National Conference of Christians and Jews. In a speech last year, he said: "Merely observing a rule or a law doesn't necessarily make one ethical. Remember, segregation laws were once legal, but most certainly obeying such laws did not make a person ethical." *Quotation*

Mr. Sand hits a nerve with that statement. Laws change, not to establish our values, but to reflect them.

For example, gambling once was widely condemned. Today, in many states, it's promoted under the guise of "revenue enhancement" through pari-mutuel betting and state lotteries. *Example*

Or consider that the sale of alcoholic beverages once was banned nationwide. Today, at most, it's restricted in some areas. . . .

. . . Maybe our society's shifting values are best illustrated in a cartoon that appeared in the *New Yorker* magazine. In that cartoon, two clean-shaven, middle-age men are sharing a jail cell. They look stiff in their new prison clothes. *Anecdote*

And one inmate says to the other, "All along, I thought our level of corruption fell well within community standards."

Ethics, then, first of all, is not merely what's enforceable. . . .

. . . James Walls is a North Carolina man whose firm provides businesses with honesty tests for job applicants. He reports that three of every 10 prospective retail workers *admit* stealing from a previous employer. *Statistics*

43

What's more, by one estimate, American workers will "steal" nearly $200 billion from their employers this year by arriving late, leaving early and misusing time on the job.

The U.S. Chamber of Commerce argues that employee theft raises the cost of consumer goods by as much as 15 percent. And a nationwide poll three years ago found that 37 percent of all taxpayers cheat.[35]

2 Back in 1945, when that Eniac computer was first powered up, it was the single-minded, driving requirement for field artillery firing tables that had made it possible.

Statistics

Could anyone looking at a 30-ton machine measuring 18 feet high and 30 feet long—containing 17,468 vacuum tubes and more than 80,000 other electronic components—have envisioned today's lightning fast supercomputers, workaholic mainframes and proliferating minis and micros?

The historical fact is that from major national efforts there are normally many related commercial developments.

Developments that raise the standard of living and advance the quality of life not just for Americans, or Europeans, or Japanese, but ultimately for all people.

Triad of Examples

That has been the contribution of this industry from the beginning. **Not just** planes of war, **but** planes of peace. **Not just** radar for defense, **but** radar to save lives and avoid disaster on land, sea and in the air. **Not just** smaller computers for space flight, **but** smaller computers to make business more efficient and life more enjoyable.[36]

3 Good morning. And thank you for inviting me to open your conference. I especially enjoy keynote speeches. The audiences are still fresh and enthusiastic...excited about seeing old friends and hearing new ideas...and as yet unaffected by the hangovers...busy slides...and the oratorical Sominex we sometimes provide you from the lectern.

I usually like to begin a keynote...therefore...on a positive...upbeat...and uplifting note. Not this morning. This morning I want to start off on a darker...more sinister...less pleasant subject...a subject that frankly disturbs and frightens me...herpetology.

Now...before any of you engineers in the audience begin squirming uncomfortably in your seats...whether from embarrassment...or...whatever reason...I should hasten to explain that herpetology is the study of reptiles...usually snakes.

Suspense

The snake I would like to talk about this morning is the boa constrictor. Now...some of you may have labored in the past under the impression that the boa constrictor drops out of a tree on its victims and quickly crushes them in the powerful folds of its body.

That is not how it operates. On the contrary...extensive research on the part of my staff...which consisted of my secretary looking up "boa constrictor" in the *Encyclopedia Americana*...has revealed the true modus operandi of this dangerous reptile. Let me read it to you.

"Ordinarily the snake places two or three coils of its body around the chest of its prey. Then...each time the victim relaxes and exhales its breath the boa simply takes up the slack. After three or four breaths there is no more slack...the

Quotation

45

prey quickly suffocates...and is then swallowed by the boa."

My fellow engineers...this deadly phenomenon of a victim becoming an unwitting accomplice in its own destruction is not confined to the animal world. Virtually all of us whose careers and ambitions depend on the efficiency and survivability of factories and manufacturing processes have seen it in action over the past several years.

The big boa we are facing...or rather failing to face...is the aggressive...hungry...efficient off-shore competition...and each coil of the snake is another recession.

Examples

One coil slipped around the steel industry...another around autos...another around cameras...consumer electronics...all accompanied by a chorus of groans and moans and heroic resolutions and jingoist rhetoric. But much of that clamor is now strangely silent.

All of a sudden the sun has come out...the market's up...employment is up...inventories are down...and what do we see in many of our key industries? A sigh of relief...and business as usual. Bonuses for the bosses and psychedelic wage demands from the unions. We're congratulating each other on a recovery we did nothing to deserve. And like Scarlett O'Hara...on

Quotation

the subject of productivity...our attitude is: "I won't worry about that today. I'll worry about it tomorrow."

Analogy

And the boa constrictor smiles as we relax once again.

Ladies and gentlemen...I've been looking forward to talking to you today because you...more than anyone...are closer to...and understand...the nature of the battle that is looming in all industries that manufacture and assemble things...over the next few years. The issue boils down to whether American manufacturing will be able to survive the combination of cheap labor and sophisticated manufacturing technology that faces us...not just from Japan...but from places like Korea...Brazil...Malaysia...Taiwan and scores of other nations.

We read about the titanic battles over the 64K RAM...and...of course...autos and steel...and computers...but there is...as well...a vast...and...I believe...more important battlefield in the less exciting...more mature...manufacturing and assembly operations many of you...and I...can't do without.[37]

Examples

4 **I know about** the teacher whose heart is filled with anger and selfishness, who can no longer be a servant. **I know about** the teacher with a meager mind, who has been allowed to slip into our classrooms without the mental power to lead and inspire. The lights are on but no one is at home. **I know about** the teacher with hardened heart, whose arrogance will never open the doors of curiosity and devotion in the mind and heart of his or her students. **I know about** the teacher who is putting in time rather than devotion, who is such a mechanic that he or she could be replaced by a computer with far more promising results. **I know about** the teacher whose mediocre expectations amount to an act of educational malpractice.

Examples introduced by "I know about. . ."

Rightly done, teaching is a precious work. It is, however, the one human endeavor most damaging in consequence when done without care or competence. To carry a student in harm's way because of either ignorance or arrogance— because we do not know or do not care—is an act far worse than a bungled surgery. Our mis-

Analogy

takes will not bleed. Instead, they carry hidden scars whose mean and tragic consequence may not be seen until years have passed and remedy is painful and impossible.

Wasted minds left dispirited, disaffected, and disengaged by those who have not been called to a journey of the heart, who have no love for learning or learners, who would touch a life forever with cruel and miserable consequence— I know about those teachers.

But the beauty and power of the loving teacher—that is the greatest instrument for good in our society. The voices of my teachers at Memphis State—what did they teach me about what it means to be an educated human being...

- To understand that perseverance and courage are more important than perfection.
- To recognize that educated men enjoy four pleasures—of which learning is the first. The other three are loving, serving, and creating. . . .

Examples

- To exhibit humility but to resist those daily assaults that wear away the beautiful edges of personality, working to make us smooth little pebbles that rub against each other without friction or meaning.
- To respect dissent and defeat as instruments of learning and self discovery but let neither dissent nor defeat take from me the power of an optimistic spirit.
- To know that behind every arrival there is a ragged journey marked with failure and defeat, that pain is the mother of compassion, that correction is the author of wisdom, that in seeds of doubt are sown the flowers of faith.
- To look for opportunity and growth in the interruptions of life.

- To understand that action informs thought, that creativity favors boldness.
- To look behind the quiet smile of my neighbor and learn what battles of conscience and conviction may rage there.
- To appreciate that there is a low road to morality—we do what is right because we fear an audit of our behavior or the reprisal of those whom we cheat of property or promise—and that there is a high road to morality—we do what is right because we have compassion and principle. . . .

Examples

- To know that technique will always be slave to purpose, that what I believe will always rule what I know. . . .
- To retreat not into the womb of ethical neutrality and irresponsibility when moral dilemma and complexity stress mind and heart, but to face squarely the call of honor, justice, and compassion.[38]

Analogy

5 Have you ever seen a volcanic eruption? It's a once-in-a-lifetime experience. We had our own Mt. St. Helens at the New York Stock Exchange last month. On Wednesday, August 18th, the tape shot past the historical and psychological 100 million share milestone and never looked back. By 4 o'clock when the market closed, the Exchange had traded a mind-boggling 133 million shares. You should have been there. It was a day you'd remember for the rest of your life.

Analogy

Let me see if I can recreate some of the excitement for you. Monday, August 16th, was a normal day. Summer doldrums. The last two weeks in August are the traditional dog days. No one expected much. The previous week had seen the Dow sink to 776, a 27-month low. It looked like some stocks would never stop going down. That's what it was like on Monday, August 16th, when we did a mere 55 million shares.

Things began to break on Tuesday. The Fed had taken another cut in the discount rate. Congress had passed President Reagan's tax package. Banks lowered their interest rates to the lowest levels in two years. Everyone began to suspect that the recession might be bottoming out, and that the economy might be picking up.

Statistics

The pace began to quicken on Tuesday. Volume was 92.8 million shares. That was just 100,000 short of the all-time record set on January 7, 1981.

You remember that day. The day when market guru Joe Granville told everyone to sell? And sell they did.

But every year has a different market guru. This year it was Henry Kaufman of Salomon Brothers. He became bullish on interest rates and predicted that they would decline even further. Kaufman set off a running of the bulls. It was as if he fired the starting gun for the Boston Marathon. The herd instinct took over.

Analogy

By the morning of Wednesday, August 18th, we all knew something big was afoot. How big we didn't know. The market opened at 10 a.m. in a frenzy of trading. By the end of the first hour we'd set a new volume record of 37 million shares. By noon we'd set a second hour record of 65.6 million shares. Upstairs in the Exchange, the phones began ringing off their hooks in our news bureau. The press was calling in from all over the world. Everyone wanted to know: "What's going on? Will we do 100 million shares?" We could only tell them we didn't know for sure. When the market moves, we are all innocent bystanders.

Statistics

On the floor, it was controlled pandemonium by one o'clock when 84 million shares had been executed. Of course, everything is relative. Computers really don't make that much noise.

By 1:30 every reporter and TV and radio crew in New York was camped at the Exchange. They—and the rest of the world—wanted to know: "Is this it?"

Quotation

Meanwhile, word leaked out to the Street. Crowds formed outside the visitors gallery. Inside, the Exchange staff began crowding into the elevators to go down and have a look. No one wanted to miss what was sure to be an historic moment.

The countdown began. 1:40 p.m.: We'd broken Joe Granville's record and passed 93 million shares! It was "Goodbye Joe Granville." All systems were still "Go." 1:45 p.m.: 95 million. 1:50 p.m.: 98 million. TV cameramen turned on their lights. Reporters began readying their microphones. Suddenly—at 1:55 p.m.—we broke through the Maginot Line of 100 million shares!

Analogy

By the time the market closed that Wednesday, we'd done a phenomenal 133 million shares. The first broker to come off the trading floor was cornered by the press. "How do you feel?" they asked him.

The exhausted fellow replied: "It was the best day of my life."

Anecdote

Amazingly, this was not the end, but just the beginning. . . ." [39]

STEP 4
Meet Again with the Speaker

M eet again with the speaker to get more ideas for supporting material and share some of the ideas you have already developed. Reconfirm the speech purpose, thesis and outline of the speech body. Both of you must be on the same wavelength.

Use this opportunity to bring to life some of the material you've gathered. See what appeals most to the speaker. Look to develop new ideas and insights. Zero in on supporting material that you think you want to use.

At this stage, you've already done a tremendous amount of work. You've analyzed the audience, met with the speaker to put together a solid plan, and armed yourself with at least three or more times the amount of supporting material you'll need. You've met a second time with the speaker and reconfirmed the basics of the speech and discussed the supporting material you've discovered. Yet you haven't written a word of the speech. That means you're on track. Now—and only now—does the writing phase begin.

REVIEW

Planning The Speech

I. Analyze the audience and occasion

II. Meet with the speaker to develop outline
    A. Discuss the Audience and Occasion
    B. Discuss topic and purpose
    C. Develop thesis
    D. Develop main points
    E. Develop subpoints

III. Research the Supporting Material
    A. Test the effectiveness of supporting material
    B. Use Examples
    C. Use Statistics
    D. Use Anecdotes
    E. Use Testimony
    F. Use Analogies

IV. Meet Again with the Speaker

PART II

WRITING THE SPEECH

STEP 1
Write the Body
of the Speech

Write the body of the speech first, beginning with the first main point. Write for the ear, though, not for the eye. The speech is being written to be heard, not to be read.

Always remember that the ear is a weak, untrained sensor. It needs all the help it can get. The speaker's listeners are going to *hear* the speech, not *read* it. That's why any speech must be written to be heard.

The most common mistake many speakers make is trying to cover too much ground in one speech. This results in a speech without focus. The second most common mistake is writing for the eye instead of the ear.

Oral writing is conversational and straightforward. It calls for short or small words, familiar words, the active voice as much as possible, active verbs, contractions, personal pronouns, and subject-verb-object order in sentences. Even incomplete sentences that still convey meaning are quite acceptable. They work.

Always keep in mind that a reader can absorb at leisure but a listener cannot. Your listeners must know exactly what you mean or how you feel when you say it. They must understand instantly. Select words and word combinations that say exactly what you mean.

The shorter the words and the more familiar the words, the more easily you will be understood, as in this advice by Joseph Ecclesine writing in *Printer's Ink* magazine:

> Small words can be brief, crisp, terse—go to the point, like a knife. They have a charm all their own. They dance, twist, turn, sing. Like sparks in the night they light the way. They are the grace notes. You know what they say the way you know a day is bright and fair. Small words move with ease where big words stand still—or, worse, bog down and get in the way of what you want to say. There is not much, in truth, that small words will not say—and say quite well.

Although the passage was written to be read, not listened to, it is excellent advice for choosing words in a speech. If read aloud, the passage also sounds pleasing to the ear because it is written in a good oral style.

Three words appear time and again in the literature on language usage in speeches: Clear, vivid, and appropriate. Using clear, simple, easy to understand language does not mean the ideas you present are going to be simplistic. Rather, it means that your ideas will be more easily understood. That's the objective.

Vivid language appeals to the senses. When the audience can see, feel, taste, hear, and smell a speaker's ideas, they will more easily understand and remember them.

If your language is clear and vivid and selected with the needs of the specific audience and occasion in mind, it will pass the test of appropriateness.

Oral Style Examples

Here are some examples from executive speeches that illustrate a good oral style. Read them out loud. Notice that they incorporate several characteristics mentioned above as well as other rhetorical devices like repetition which are covered in the next section.

1 Here we are again and here we go again! **Just as I** was drafting my remarks for this conference... **Just as I** was preparing to tell you that we've come a long way since the Packard Commission report... **Just as I** was building a strong case for more self governance among contractors...Charges of alleged widespread fraud and bribery in defense-contract awards become public.

Short words

Repetition based on personal pronouns

A grand jury **gets set** to hear evidence in the wide-ranging FBI investigation of this matter. And the story is **put under** the hot white, penetrating light of the media, where it has stayed for the past five weeks.

Active verbs

Are we like Sisyphus? Eternally **pushing** the rock up the hill only to have it **roll down** again whenever it neared the top?

Analogy

61

*Personal
pronouns ,
contraction*

As American citizens, we have been attacking the problem of corruption and fraud in dealings with the government since George Washington's time. We'll keep at it forever.

During the second day of the House Armed Services Committee hearings probing weapons-buying corruption, there were calls to abandon or toughen the self-governance system that grew out of David Packard's commission findings.

*Parallel
elements,
rhetorical
questions,
sentence
fragments*

Toughen it? Yes. Abandon it? Never.

True, there are things that self governance cannot do. That laws and procedures cannot do. That audit and surveillance cannot do. That even punishment cannot do. No matter what we spend or how aggressively we attack the problem.

Anecdote

I remember how well my criminal law professor drove the point home with a famous case in early English law. The English government wanted to stamp out pickpocketing. So it announced with fair warning that the next person caught picking a pocket would be hung in the public square. The occasion of the hanging drew a huge crowd. And...you guessed it...there were more pockets picked at that hanging than had been picked the entire year.

*Sentence
fragments,
personal
pronouns,
contractions*

Granted, the latest scandal is disheartening. Disheartening to me. To you. To millions of honest hardworking people in the service of the federal government and in the employ of defense contractors nationwide. But if out of this comes further progress, rather than reaction and rehash...If our country nets out a winner...We'll all be better off despite the disillusionment we may be feeling now.

So my fervor for corporate self governance is as strong as ever. And I'm pleased to be here today to persuade you, if you're not already convinced, of its value.[40]

2 Illiteracy has reached epidemic proportions. Today, 27 million Americans, one-in-five, more than the entire population of Canada, are functional illiterates.

Statistics

That means, basically, they can exist. Like turtles on the beach. They are there—period. They can write their names—maybe. They can't read a street sign. They can't look up a phone number. They can't count change. They can't follow directions on a medicine bottle. They can't fill out a job application, to say nothing of reading a newspaper or *Huckleberry Finn*.

Analogy, short sentences, short words, subject-verb-object order, pronouns, contractions, repetition, examples

They are lost, just lost. The results are tragic and widespread.

In Illinois, a farm hand recently destroyed an entire herd of cattle when he mistook poison for feed.

A child was rushed to a New York Hospital when her mother thought the liquid dish washing soap was antacid.

A seaman off the coast damaged a quarter-million dollars worth of equipment because he couldn't read the instructions.

Examples

And that's not unique. The Navy has found 30 percent of its recruits a danger to themselves and to costly equipment because they cannot understand the instructions.

Certainly, the personal cost of inadequate education is beyond estimation. The social cost is estimated at a whopping $225 billion annually—in welfare checks, crime, job incompetence, lost taxes and remedial education.

Statistics

It has been the focus of countless hours and hand-wringing testimony, of endless seminars

Statistics

and scores of books. It has been a source of international disgrace. Of the 158 United Nations members, the U.S. ranks an embarrassing 49th in literacy.

Most astounding is that many illiterates have completed high school: 12 years of reading, writing and arithmetic and they can't select a movie for Saturday night.[41]

Sentence Fragments

Analogy

Active verbs

3 Intrapreneurialism. One minute management. Strategic alliances. Leveraged recapitalizations. Right-brain thinking.

These are some of the exotic plants that **grow** in management's magic garden. This garden has rich soil, the kind of loam that has **generated** fads—and confusion—throughout history.

The fertilizer that **feeds** the magical garden is profound anxiety resulting from unprecedented global competition, and the economic and social upheaval it has brought about in many industries.

The herbs and flowers that **grow** in this garden look and **smell** wonderful to us, and so we harvest and compound them into magical management pills. They are easy to **swallow**; but they can be "bad medicine," panaceas that give us a false sense of comfort while failing entirely to address the organic ills that cause organizational distress. I would like to suggest that instead of looking to magical "Pepto-Business" pills, we must learn to rely on our real strengths as managers—maturity, a realistic perspective, strategic focus, tenacity, and integrity—if we are really serious about revitalizing our economy.[42]

4 . . . As the engine **roared**, and the smoke stack **belched**, and the craft **shook** violently, some of the crowd **shouted** scornfully: "She'll never start!" But **off she went** up the river, with the same people—after a moment of astonished silence—**shouting** scornfully: "She'll never stop, she'll never stop!" [43]

Active verbs, short words, quotation, contractions

5 Leaders innovate. They create. They make things happen. They shape their environment. Managers tend to focus too much energy on administration. They want to do things right rather than do the right thing. . . .

Short sentences

If you want to succeed, create an atmosphere for good communication and practice it. . . . Keep your communications simple; signal effectively. . . . If you are walking through an operation and you see an unsafe act, or if you see poor housekeeping and you are the manager and do not say anything to the people around you, have you told them something? Darn right you have. You have signaled that quality is not important in your organization. What is important to you becomes important to them. . . .

Example

Be sure that you set them—standards and goals—very high and really reach out and dedicate yourself and your organization to achieving those goals. . . .

Personal pronouns

If you are not on top of your game or are not sure of what you're doing, you will not relish the idea of accountability. If this is where you are coming from, you are not going to be very comfortable in our environment because we tell people what we expect from them, give them the resources to do it, and hold them accountable for doing it. . . .

Short words

Require people to be at the top of their game. Be demanding and do not apologize for it. You build better people if you force them to understand why things are happening. Do not accept generalizations or cavalier attitudes. . . .[44]

Personal pronouns

Sentence fragments

Contractions

6 To me, writing is more an attitude than avoiding adjectives. A mind-set, instead of pondering what modifiers to use. A voice with which your company speaks, not whether to use this verb or that. It's perhaps including such with-it words as *awesome* in your first draft, as Federal Express did—but then editing out such words because they're inappropriate in an annual report...which, alas, Federal Express did not do.

Examples

Sentence fragment

Writing well for the investor is employing wordsmiths with a love of the language, the flair with words, of a Koppers in Pittsburgh, a Manufacturers Hanover in New York City, a Dow Chemical in Midland, Michigan, a Control Data in Minneapolis, a San Diego Gas & Electric on the West Coast. Enough about writing well for the investor.[45]

Personal pronouns

7 As huge a market as the United States is...as blessed as we are by natural and man-made resources...as much as we continue to hold a lead in high technology...and, as important as we are as the main pillar of defense in the free world—it is clear that we no longer enjoy the clear-cut leadership of the post-war era.

We are the world's largest debtor nation.

We are staggering under a federal budget deficit—financed by Japan and others.

We face a still stubborn trade deficit—though exports are improving as a result of the lower dollar.

And we are struggling with some very deep-seated problems in education, in commitment to R&D, and capital investment.[46]

Use Common Rhetorical Devices

Try using several of the more common rhetorical devices that are effective in oral writing: **metaphors**, **triads**, and **repetition**. These devices add force to a speech. They command attention. They help make ideas vivid and clear. They emphasize meaning. There are many others to be sure, including rhetorical questions, alliteration, and paired elements, but those listed here will probably be the most useful to you.

Metaphors

Metaphors are often an excellent source for creating vividness in language. Consider this vivid and memorable passage from a previously mentioned speech about a company's recovery. In it the chief executive officer is likened to a surgeon, a chef, and an orchestra conductor:

> The initial diagnosis is simple. The patient is dying, quite rapidly. It's time to be a surgeon and for surgery to begin at once. That means cutting manpower but keeping quality. . . .
>
> At this point you become the new chef—and there's room for only one chef in any company. The chef's job is to find the right ingredients and the proper people to cook up a strategy that will make things happen. . . .
>
> Still in the first 100 days, you change roles and become the orchestra conductor—now you bring all the people together, give them your understanding of what must be done, and then you orchestrate their efforts to get it done. . . .

Metaphor

Happy second anniversary. Surgical duties are at a minimum and the chef is in charge with the conductor doing some orchestration and waiting for the time to become a full-time performer.[47]

Or, consider this ice-skating metaphor by E. John P. Browne of the Standard Oil Production Company, in remarks on challenges global business leaders face in a changing world:

To begin, I would like to recall the recent Winter Olympics in Calgary, particularly the memorable ice skating duel between Brian Boitano of the U.S. and Brian Orser of Canada. The story behind young Mr. Boitano's triumph is worth careful consideration since it exemplified successfully meeting the challenge of change.

Metaphor

Boitano's reputation was built on absolute technical mastery, robotic precision. But he was never known for emotional skating or flair. This made the peak of skating glory elusive. Five years ago he was seventh in the World Cup. Four years ago he was fifth in the Olympics. And even though he captured the World Cup in 1985, he saw the skating world discounting his technical excellence in favor of flamboyant mannerism. So he and his long-time coach went back to the drawing board. A new, dramatic choreographer was recruited. And Brian Boitano applied himself for over a year, painfully grafting onto his technical excellence the emotional new acting style which dazzled the Calgary Olympics, and the result was a Gold Medal. Like any good manager, Brian Boitano didn't just happen. He was trained. I use his story as a metaphor for the challenge business leaders face today.

What the world wants is changing rapidly, sometimes subtly but sometimes with sledgehammer force. And things need to get done in an ever more complex environment. In his own business, Boitano looked ahead, analyzed the shifting marketplace and what might be done, made his decisions, and worked hard along a new path to success. His story also exemplified today's global economy: Boitano is an American, his choreographer is Canadian, and his marketplace is dominated by Europeans.[48]

Metaphor

Triads

Triads are groups of three. Groupings of elements in units of three are forceful, remembered, and persuasive. They can be used effectively almost anywhere in a speech. They can break unwieldy blocks of information. They're especially useful in adding emphasis when you're concluding a passage or closing a speech.

Several triads are highlighted in the following passages. As you can see, it is difficult to overuse them.

1 Thank you...good afternoon...and congratulations to each and every one of you. Now, I know it's a little unusual to start off a speech by congratulating the audience, but in this case, the shoe really fits. You see, it's you—the business community of Grand Rapids...and everyone you've been able to **catalyze** and **motivate** and **energize**...who have defied all the people who've appointed themselves the "morticians" of the Midwest.

Triads

They've said that our region is incapable of change. But you've shifted and diversified your business base and worked together to find new ways of generating wealth.

They've said our region is slipping into an irreversible decline. But Grand Rapids is a center of growth and vitality. To mention just a couple of examples close to home...a $100 million expansion of GM's Rochester Products Plant and a $500 million expansion of our C-P-C Stamping Plant are well under way.

And **they've said our region** has nothing to offer compared to sophisticated New York or sunny California. Well, I know as well as you that the quality of life in Grand Rapids is just superb—and your house will cost you about a fourth of what you'll pay in those other places.

So, yes, Grand Rapids, my hat's off to you. This is one city that's learned that change is the only thing that's permanent. And you've learned **to live with it...to like it...**and **to make a success of it.** In a sense, we're kindred spirits— because that is exactly what we're doing at GM.

Triads

And that brings me right to my subject for today. It's something that's on a lot of people's minds—yours too, I would imagine: the American auto industry and General Motor's role in it. You've been reading and hearing quite a bit about GM's fortunes lately. That's partly a function of your being here in Michigan. And it's partly a result of the fact that we're so large that almost anything we do is bound to affect a great many people.

I'm going to tell you a story that sounds like some others you've heard—from the newspapers, from TV, maybe from your friend or neighbor who has some connection with us or with our business. The crucial difference between my presentation and theirs, however, is this: today you're going to get the inside perspective. **Others may wonder whether** GM knows where it's going. **I know that** it does.

Others may wonder whether our products can grab and excite and satisfy our customers. **I know that** they can—and do. **Others may wonder whether** GM is doing what's best for its own long-term growth and for the economic health of our country. **I know that** it is.[49]

2 Our people **need to** care. Our customers **need to** know that we care. General managers **need to** think of customer service as an investment—a win—not as an expense or a nuisance. Examine the worst airline you can think of next to the best you can think of, and it is readily apparent that the difference is not in organization—systems compensation—marketing or anything else. The difference is that one airline has a culture that cares, that reflects a total commitment to customer service—and the other does not. Laying organizational planks over a culture that does not revere the customer almost religiously is piling them on quicksand.[50]

Triads

3 What you have **discussed, argued** and **resolved** here could have a profound influence on your communities and this nation for generations to come.

For you have sent a message **to the administration** in Washington and **to the governments** in your state houses and town halls and **to the business leadership** of your communities.

And the message is this. Business is ready to take on the new initiatives this administration has made possible. It is ready to use **its resources, its talents** and **its skills,** to do what needs to be done to create a stronger economy and a better life for the people of this nation.

For five decades now, business has told "big government" that there are better ways of doing things than proliferating the bureaucracy and throwing money at problems.

We have said, **"Give us a chance to prove what we can do."**

For five decades, the states and communities of America have said to Washington, "We know better than you how to solve the social and economic problems on our own doorsteps. **Give us the chance to prove what we can do."**

Triads

For five decades, business has said to the people of America, "We care about the quality of life in this country. We want a bigger share in improving the process of education, of training, of transportation, and of getting essential services to the public. **Give us a chance to prove what we can do."**

The time has come. The chance is now. A new president has made a major change in the direction of America. America is on a new course. There is a new philosophy. Ronald Reagan supports the doctrine of "free enterprise" and local control. He really believes that private enterprise can solve the problems and capitalize on the opportunities before us. He is shrinking the federal budget. He has reduced taxes. He is encouraging savings. He is slashing the bureaucracy and the federal presence that has loomed so large in our lives.

This administration has said what we have been waiting to hear for so long, **"If it can be done** at the local level, do it. **If it can be done** by private initiative, do it. **If it can be done** by individual effort and personal commitment, do it." [51]

Repetition

Repetition doesn't mean repeating yourself. Repetition in speechwriting is a repeated phrase, word or words at the beginning, middle, or end of a sentence, clause or phrase. Repetition can add punch to your ideas.

Don't confuse repetition with "restatement," which is simply rephrasing a point or idea in different words for emphasis or recall. Restating the main points of a speech, for example, is commonly used in the conclusion.

In the first example below, repetition is used at the beginning of successive sentences. In the second, at the beginning and internally. In the third, it is used internally. The key words are highlighted. As with triads, it is difficult to over-use repetition.

1 You are the best ambassadors in our communities that a newspaper could have. Classifieds are a great national institution.

We find jobs and job seekers together—reducing unemployment and boosting income levels. **We** find apartments for those newly arrived in our communities. And **we** put young couples into their first homes. **We** are a great conservator of national resources—by helping people to recycle their possessions. One person gains some money and more space in the garage; another gets the item he or she needed at lower cost.

Think of all the things in this nation that repeatedly change hands instead of being thrown away. **We** help keep the cost of living down for folks. **We** also keep our nation's

Repetition

landfills and incinerators from being choked with castoffs.

We also—through the classified pages—provide a daily market report on the value of a family's investment in possessions—bicycles, the old automobile, the lawn mower, or that "antique" piece of furniture. All can be turned into cash or other possessions through our great marketplace of the people.[52]

2 **To all those companies** that are nervous about diving into markets overseas **I say,** come on in, the water's fine once you get used to it. It is worth the effort.

Repetition

To the consumers of America **I say**, American products are getting better all the time. **Our** automobiles are at the leading edge of technology, thanks in part to *Du Pont* materials. **Our** textiles, **our** sports equipment, **our** planes, **our** boats, **our** pharmaceuticals, **our** electronics, **our** agricultural products—all these American things—are world class. Try us, you'll like us.

To all our governments—federal, state, and local—**I say,** before you pass one more law, consider its possible effect on the business climate and on the ability of American businesses to compete in the global marketplace of which we are all a part.

To the federal government, **I say**, go ahead—intervene. But remember, there are many means of intervention.[53]

3 We've **lost** our unrivaled technological edge; **lost** our virtual monopoly on best quality; lost our lower capital costs and **lost** our superior rate of productivity growth. . . .

So the situation has **changed...changed** completely...and **changed** permanently...but not necessarily **changed** for worse. Time has not run out. The point is that it's up to us not only to understand that change is here for good—but to make sure it's here for better.[54]

Repetition

REVIEW

Planning The Speech

I. Analyze the audience and occasion

II. Meet with the speaker to develop outline
   A. Discuss the audience and occasion
   B. Discuss topic and purpose
   C. Develop thesis
   D. Develop main points
   E. Develop subpoints

III. Research the supporting material
   A. Test the effectiveness of supporting material
   B. Use examples
   C. Use statistics
   D. Use anecdotes
   E. Use testimony
   F. Use analogies

IV. Meet again with the speaker

Writing The Speech

I. Write the body of the speech
- A. Oral style
- b. Metaphors
- C. Triads
- D. Repetition

STEP 2
Write
the Introduction

Write the introduction next. The introduction should gain attention, establish credibility and goodwill, and preview the speech body for which you've already written a draft. The thesis or central idea will be a part of the introduction unless it's merely implied in the speech.

Any kind of supporting material previously mentioned is appropriate for use in the introduction. Put yourself on the other side of the lectern and think about what would really grab your attention. Would a vivid metaphor do it? Would three or four factual, undetailed, startling examples really capture your attention? Would a striking analogy work best?

Everyone has one truly great joke, one great anecdote, or one great story which has been stored up for just the right occasion. Invariably, this gem will not fit in the opening of the speech. It will not fit anywhere in the speech. Yet the writer or the speaker will persist and bend and torture the structure of the speech so that this particular darling can be included. Be ruthless when it comes to using that favorite joke or bit of inspirational poetry or quotation. Like everything else, it can be included only if it fits the audience and the occasion and relates directly to the subject.

The following exemplify excellent speech introductions.

Suspense

1 Tonight I want to talk about something that's been around ever since we human beings first gathered together into tribes. In fact, society would be impossible without it. Over the centuries some of our best thinkers have been absolutely fascinated by it. There are probably as many theories about it as there are theorists. And today we need it more than ever.

Analogy

I'm talking about leadership. One writer said that trying to analyze it is like studying the Abominable Snowman: you see the footprints...but never the thing itself. Nevertheless, in the next few minutes, I'd like to offer some thoughts on what it is...and on the kind of leadership that we need in America today.

Personal pronouns, contractions

I certainly don't pretend to have mastered this enormous subject, but I do have some first-hand experience with it, and I've done a lot of thinking about it over the years. And my basic conclusion is this: new competitive conditions...and the changing nature of leadership itself call for a new kind of business leadership that changes individuals within GM—and eventually, transforms the entire organization.

How do I arrive at that? Let me start my answer by touching briefly on the conditions that define business leadership in the 1980s. . . .[55]

Rhetorical question

2 I was invited here to speak of "change," and not long after I received your kind invitation, a small newspaper story caught my eye. Its headline read, "Iceberg twice as big as Rhode Island breaks away from coast of Antarctica."

It seems that in one awesome moment last month, a 2,500-square-mile chunk of ice **cracked** free from the continent and began to **drift** away. In that one instant, all our maps became obsolete...the Bay of Whales was **doomed** to disappear...and we were given a rare glimpse of how geological time, which we usually only **ponder** in the abstract, can elapse...in a heartbeat. Now, folks...if you want to talk about change—well, that's change!

Analogy

Active verbs

Short words

How did it happen? Nothing earth shattering, really. No earthquakes, no tidal waves. What happened was this: Almost invisible forces at work for a long, long, time coalesced at the proper moment to change an apparently immutable mass. Engineers with dynamite probably couldn't have done it, but the patient, methodical forces of trickling water—individual drops, converging and working together as one body—eventually helped carve that 2,500-square-mile ice cube apart and set it free.

Rhetorical question, sentence fragment

As we gather to think about education, it strikes me that our challenge here in the South seems almost as formidable as that polar icecap...and that educational progress...change for the better, if you will...seems at times to move at only glacial speed.

Personal pronouns

Analogy

Does that sound pessimistic? Well, yes, it does. But the truth is, I'm an optimist. Now—don't get

Short words, personal pronouns, contractions, repetition

me wrong. I'm not here to tell you things are rosy. **You know** Johnny can't read—**you know** better than I do, in fact, because **you know** Johnny better than I do. You've seen him grow up and drop out of your schools.

And **we all know** Johnny's dragging the rest of us down. **We all know** we do have deeply disturbing educational problems in the New South. And I don't deny that even with consid- erable public resources, our government, alone, cannot stem the tide **of** illiteracy...**of** dropouts...**of** the perpetual underclass...**of** the real, flesh-and-blood problems whose taproots are...our educational shortcomings.

Repetition ("we all know" and "of")

Yet I'm cautiously encouraged despite all the grim news. Why? **It's because** I see imaginative support for education reform trickling in from new quarters. **It's because** I believe enough individual drops of water can collectively carve and reshape a continent. **It's because** I believe in the South we've finally reached critical mass, at long last—we finally in the South seem to care enough about the problem to fix it.[56]

Triad ("It's because...")

Metaphor

Personal pronouns, contrac- tions, per- sonal anecdote

3 It's good to be back in Indiana and particu- larly in Kokomo. Some of the most interesting and exciting years of my GM career were spent here. I have to admit, though, my time in Indiana didn't start all that auspiciously. I'd been working in Milwaukee for several years when I was offered a position at Allison in Indianapolis. Our son was in the seventh grade and our daughter had just entered high school. They were very much against the move—as you can imagine. My wife and I talked to them about it, and finally one night our son said, "Look, dad. We're going to give up our home, our friends, everything we like. I know it's better for you, but what happens if you blow it?" I guess your toughest critic isn't always your boss.

Shortly after I became general manager of Delco Electronics, I was attending a picnic that the division holds every year for retirees. As part of the festivities, the oldest living retiree present receives an award. And to determine the oldest living retiree, they ask all those over 45 to stand, then they ask the people over 76 to remain standing, and so forth.

Anecdote

The first year I attended the picnic, I sat next to a lady who was 89 years old. She—of course—remained standing while the judges moved up the age categories. In fact, it got to the point that only this 89-year-old lady and a gentleman were left standing. Finally, the judges asked the 89-year-olds to sit down.

My neighbor sat down, the gentleman remained standing and was awarded his prize. The lady turned to me and said, "Darn him, he wins every year." I guess she thought she was catching up.

Sometimes we Americans stop to look around at the world, and we're surprised at what we see. Unlike the gentleman in the contest, we have the feeling that the world is catching up with us. And that's not a pleasant feeling for people who are used to being in the forefront of everything.

Analogy

We find ourselves in the midst of revolutionary change—change that affects not only U.S. industry but all of America and its business and economic relations with the rest of the world. This new industrial revolution is characterized by the emergence of a fiercely competitive global economy.

The auto industry is a good example of how worldwide competition is changing. Today, GM, Ford, and Chrysler—the domestically owned

Example

Statistics

companies—account for about 68 percent of the U.S. passenger car market—down from 84 percent in 1975 and 94 percent in 1965.

Twelve manufacturers—including 9 from overseas—have at least a one-percent share of U.S. car sales. In 1965—only 22 years ago—only one overseas competitor—Volkswagen—had a share of the U.S. market that exceeded one percent.

Unfortunately, much of the American business community has not responded to this new environment as well as we might have hoped. American business appears to be losing its competitive edge. And that should be a matter of serious concern to all of us. For ultimately, if American industry is not competitive, everyone in this country will be affected.

During the next few minutes, I shall discuss the problems associated with the declining competitiveness of American industry and the approach I believe we must follow to fix them.[57]

Paraphrase

4 Thank you, Stuart, for that all too generous introduction. If, as Mark Twain said, a man can live a month on one compliment, you have just assured me of immortality. You will go to heaven for your charity, unless you go somewhere else for your exaggerations.

I am grateful for those kind words and for this opportunity to talk with you today.

Anecdote

Lyndon Johnson was forever trying to do his colleagues "one better." For example, it seems that when he was in the Senate, as majority leader, he used to take great pleasure teasing Everett Dirksen about LBJ's newest toy, a car telephone.

Every night when Johnson left for home, he saw Ev Dirksen still at work, so he called him up from his car telephone and would say, "Guess where I am calling you from, Ev?" And the answer would always be the same: "From my car telephone."

Well, one day disgusted with this, Dirksen got himself a car phone, and when he saw Johnson leaving the building, he ran down to his car and, before Johnson could place his call, he called LBJ. "Guess where I am calling you from, Lyndon?" said Dirksen. "Where?" inquired the future president. "From my car phone!" replied Dirksen. There was a brief pause, then LBJ, never to be outdone, said, "Just a minute, Ev, my *other* phone is ringing!"

Well, that is the way I feel as I look at your program. You could not do better, and your conference planning staff are to be congratulated. . . .[58]

5 "The reasonable man adapts himself to the world. The unreasonable one persists in trying to adapt the world to himself. Therefore all progress depends on the unreasonable man."

Quotation

Good morning. I'm Al Warren. Those were the words of the famous British writer George Bernard Shaw.

This morning I want to ask you to be unreasonable people. Now, when I tell you to be unreasonable I'm not suggesting that you go home and get in trouble with your parents—or with the school officials—or the local law enforcement officers.

Personal pronouns, contractions, short words, short sentences, example

No, let me tell you what I think an unreasonable person is by using an example. The man I want to tell you about died a few years ago. He was a good friend of mine. But he's best remembered because he was a professional baseball player. His name was Vic Wertz.

Unless you're such an avid baseball fan that you've checked up on old timers, most of you probably don't remember Vic. He played for the Detroit Tigers and some other major league teams. And he had a pretty respectable career: a lifetime batting average of .277; he batted in 1,351 runs, and hit 266 home runs. In the 1954 World Series, he had a hit that would have been a home run, if Willie Mays hadn't made a spectacular catch.

But none of that made Vic an "unreasonable man." What made him "unreasonable" was a disease. In the middle of his baseball career, Vic Wertz came down with polio. For most "reasonable" people an attack of polio would mean the end of a major league career. But not for Vic! He fought back. And with plenty of hard work and determination, he resumed his career.

Inspirational anecdote

And after his baseball career ended, he embarked on a new career as a businessman—running an extremely successful beer distributorship in Mt. Clemens. The Miller Brewing Company named Vic a "Miller Master" several times for his excellence in all aspects of running his company.

But even successful athletic and business careers weren't enough for Vic. He also sponsored golf tournaments for the benefit of the Boys and Girls Clubs. He started snowmobile races to raise money for the Special Olympics and a hospital bed race to benefit Easter Seals.

Vic was a talented athlete. You don't make it to the majors without talent. But he had that something extra—that "unreasonable" attitude of grit and determination that carried over into everything he did.

And I'd like to suggest to you that "unreasonable" people—like Vic—do particularly well in the American system.[59]

STEP 3
Write the Conclusion

Now write the conclusion. It essentially restates the substance of the speech and focuses on the speaker's desired response. It should leave the listeners with a sense of completion. In the case of a persuasive speech, the speaker must issue a call to action or state clearly what must be done and by whom. A good approach is to summarize the main points in different words and leave the audience with a memorable and emphatic closer—an anecdote, quotation or observation.

It is well to read aloud your thesis statement and think of your closing as a variation of it—in more emphatic language. It is the place in a speech to use some of the strongest elements of style, particularly the triad, the paired contrast, repetition, and short words.

A classic combination that achieves this strong emphasis involves the use of triads and paired elements. In this example, the triad repeats the phrase "it will take" and the paired contrast takes the form of *"THIS not THAT"*:

> But it will take sacrifice; it will take forbearance; and, it will certainly take a consistent concern for productivity and investment. In short, it will take action, not words.[60]

In the next example, repetition of "Let's," a paired contrast *("NOT only . . . BUT")* and a final rhetorical question make for another brief and effective conclusion:

> Let's monitor performance, let's complain when promises are broken, let's use our electoral muscle to get the sort of government we deserve. Let's work to get more women elected to public office. Let's humanize government—to make it not only accountable, but responsive, to the people who elected it.
>
> After all, who deserves it more than we do? [61]

The following examples illustrate the use of a variety of devices used in conclusions. Each one is effective in its own way and leaves the audience with a sense of finality.

Rhetorical questions, sentence fragments, personal pronouns, repetition

1 Can the entrepreneur survive in large companies? Certainly. But only if those companies remember that size and security are not ends unto themselves. Large companies should take heed not to let their sheer size crush entrepreneurs.

Where will we find tomorrow's entrepreneurs? By looking into the mirror. By accepting the need for risk. By realizing that we must accommodate ourselves to the entrepreneur, and not vice versa.

If we go back to our business and preach, cajole—fight, if necessary—in support of entrepreneurship, we just may produce a light so bright that it will cast away the darkness.[62]

Paired elements ("If...then"), metaphor

2 All of these challenges therefore require an extra dosage of good old American ingenuity, discipline, patience, stronger commitment and hard work to regain competitiveness—those characteristics our grandfathers said were the keys to prosperity in the 19th century. We need to relearn those basic lessons to survive the 20th century and to begin the 21st.

However ironic it may sound, we should be thankful that the Japanese arrived on our shores when they did and showed us: **That** 90 percent quality was not good enough. **That** we shouldn't accept fixed goals/targets. **That** employee involvement is key. The long-term/short-term balance.

Triad, short words, sentence fragments

Unfortunately, the talk and the headlines are too often about the seductive macroeconomic solutions—monetary policy, industrial policy, trade policies—and the generic trendy business solutions—corporate culture, 60 minute MBAs, and so on. Certainly, we need more private R&D investment, improved education, greater tax incentives, removal of antitrust barriers to research, reduction of the federal deficit and improved export incentives.

Examples

However, in the meantime, and even thereafter, the reality is that the real competitiveness takes place on the individual firm level, where actions are controllable and where real wealth is created.

Emphasis gained through use of paired contrast	**Individual companies, not government,** are the lifeblood of American competitiveness. Our short history of two centuries has shown that Americans again and again are most resilient and ingenious when faced with threats to our survival. It will never be in our best interest to banish foreign competitors from our markets.
Triad	U.S. management will find its greatest security by maintaining an environment of insecurity. To succeed, we need continuous challenge from foreign competitors. Competition doesn't contribute to failure. Poor management **does.** Lack of vision **does.** Inability to make hard decisions **does.**
Paired contrast ("not only...but"), short words, metaphor	I'm confident that we will not only become more competitive in this global market, but that we will succeed in new markets that are yet to appear. We will create new games as well as learn how to play the old games better. [63]

3 Tort litigation has and surely will in the future drive some bad products off the market, but for every step forward, tort liability has, and can only continue, to force us to take two steps back.

Repetition

Across the board, the message to scientists, engineers, doctors and pharmacologists is this: **Don't** innovate, **don't** experiment, **don't** be venturesome, **don't** go out on a limb. A legal system that persistently sends such a message to the technological community as ours has been

Metaphor

doing, is sowing the seeds for national disintegration. Repeated sufficiently often, this anti-innovation message may yet bring an end to the great American experiment as predicted by T. S.

Paraphrase

Eliot. It is still all too possible that our world will end not with a bang, which the apocalyptics like to predict, but with a whimper as our technology falls finally and irretrievably behind the technologies of other countries.

Is the liability nightmare over? Yes, I suppose it is. Most insurers survived the crisis of '84 and '85 by selling much less insurance at vastly higher prices. Most major industrial concerns and doctors and drug companies survived by selling nasal sprays instead of vaccines. Yes, the nightmare is over, but the question is whether we are in a technological coma instead. The signs are increasing that we may well be.[64]

Metaphor

Example

Metaphor

4 We need to be like the hero in a play by Tom Stoppard called "The Real Thing." In the first scene of act two, the playwright has the hero, who is a writer, say these words about words:

"Words are innocent, neutral, precise...standing for this...describing that...meaning the other. So if you look after them, you can build bridges across incomprehension and chaos. I don't think writers are sacred...words are. They deserve respect. If you get the right ones in the right order, you can nudge the world a little or make a poem which children will speak for you when you're dead."

Quotation

This year I hope we can nudge PRSA [Public Relations Society of America], our profession and ourselves more than a little toward making this a better place for all of us.[65]

5 Since the mid-seventies, many foreign governments have looked on deregulation of U.S. airlines with great skepticism. But while those governments have been **criticizing, chastising and challenging** the United States, they have also been watching.

Triad

*Triad of
examples*

And something's happened in the last three years. The **Canadians** are exploring deregulation. The **Australians** are exploring deregulation. And even some **Europeans** are exploring deregulation.

*Personal
pronouns,
contractions,
triad, short
words*

They are learning what we have known since the time of buggy whips and whale oil. The free market works, if we let it work. And it's beginning to work in trucking, banking, energy and communications.

But with that freedom comes a responsibility. If business becomes **indifferent**, if we become **lazy**, if we become **greedy**, the public outcry for re-regulation will be deafening and nothing will silence it. To be free, we must be responsible.

The choice is ours, and that's the way it should be.[66]

6 She is a special lady to all of us, and we honor her tonight...because she **remembers,** and because she helps all of us **remember**.

*Metaphor,
active verbs,
repetition of
"remember"*

Exactly ninety-nine years ago today, a beautiful lady **dressed** in 200 tons of copper and iron **stood** staring through the mist in New York harbor, a little like a blushing bride. Quite a fuss was made over her that day. Cannons **roared**, brass bands **played,** all the ships in the harbor **blew** their whistles and **rang** their bells.

She was that day a young symbol of an old but elusive dream—the simple ideal of "liberty." Tonight, ninety-nine years later but forever young, she stands not only for that original ideal itself, but also as a symbol of what free people, guided and protected by that ideal, can achieve.

For as soon as the cannons and the bands were silent, she began to see the ships slipping into the harbor with the first of the millions of immigrants she would welcome to America.

Tonight she **remembers** those ships coming from Bremen and Liverpool and Naples...and the cargo they brought. Human beings seeking refuge and opportunity beneath her torch.

Vivid phrasing

They all stood on deck in their best clothes...clutching the kids, and maybe an old cardboard suitcase with a rope around it. It was the biggest day of their lives.

Triad ("backs," "faces," "eyes")

And as the ships went by her on their way to Ellis Island, a lot of **backs**, bent by oppression, began to straighten. And a lot of **faces**, scarred by tyranny, were suddenly smiling. And a lot of **eyes**, dimmed by despair, began to glow with hope.

She saw all that, and **she remembers** it well tonight.

Repetition of "she," "they," "remember"

She remembers, too, what happened to them after they passed beyond her gaze.

She kept her promise of liberty, but it wasn't the liberty of streets paved with gold. It was the **liberty** of the shovel, the **freedom** of the push-cart, and the **dignity** of the plow.

Triad ("liberty," "freedom," "dignity")

It was the freedom to work hard, and to keep what that hard work built.

They were ambitious in a time when ambition was not a dirty word.

They were hardworking in a time when hard work was not something to be avoided.

Short words, short sentences

They were builders.

They built a country.

And what **they** built was the America we have today—imperfect, but better by far than anything anybody else has ever built, anywhere.

The Lady **remembers** how **they** did it, and so should we.

They did it with pain, and sweat and tears.

You know, **America isn't great** because of its natural resources. **It's great because** those people dug into the ground, often under terrible conditions, and took the resources out.

Repetition of paired elements ("America isn't great" . . . It's great because")

America isn't great because of miles of open prairies. **It's great because** people broke their backs to bust the sod and grow food.

America isn't great because of a few industrial geniuses. **It's great because** of the thousands of others who fired the furnaces and forged the metal.

And America isn't great because of a piece of paper called a Constitution. **It's great because** people fought, and bled, and sometimes died to fulfill its promise of a just and humane society.

So, the Lady **remembers**, if sometimes we forget. She **remembers** who we are and where we came from.

We're all her children...whether she saw our people arrive on those ships from Europe...or whether they came on the Mayflower...or from Africa in chains...or from the Far East or Latin America.

Repetition and short words

She is a special lady to all of us, and we honor her tonight...because she **remembers**, and because she helps all of us **remember**...just what kind of people we are.[67]

Make the Right Connections... Use Coherent Transitions

Go back through the speech draft you have completed and examine how you've gone from one point or part to the next. Transitions are the coherent links that connect the various parts of the speech. Too often, they are weak or nonexistent.

Well-chosen transitions keep the speech on a smooth track. They enable the audience to easily follow the ideas being presented as well as to see the relationship of those ideas. Strong transitions help to keep the attention and interest of listeners in what is being said.

Key areas for transitions are:

- from the introduction to the body;

- from a main point to a subpoint;
- from a subpoint to a support;
- from a support to another main point;
- and from the last support under the final main point to the conclusion.

Consider these excerpts from John Bonée's speech cited earlier in the section on outlining. They demonstrate how to use transitions effectively, especially from main points to subpoints.

What are the theoretical problems you will run into when you become a speechwriter? There are at least four. The first is a prejudice in favor of logic over rhetoric, of sweet reason over emotional appeal. . . . So, one theoretical problem is a prejudice in favor of logic as against rhetoric. The second is. . . . The third problem in handling a speaker (after you've resisted the temptation to depend on reason alone and to say everything you know) is a prejudice in favor of visual aids. . . . Our fourth prejudice is a prejudice in favor of a written style. . . .

So much for the theoretical problems. Now, a few practical ones. There are three practical problems every speechwriter encounters. First, the interface between you and your speaker. . . . Another practical barrier is clearances. Everybody is an editor. . . . So, the first practical problem was interfaces, the second clearances, and there's a final one—how to merchandise the speech. . . . I've talked about the theoretical barriers and the practical problems you face in managing your relationship with the speaker. They are. . . .[68]

Commonly Used Transitions

Here are number of commonly used transitions to trigger your thoughts should you have difficulty connecting ideas in the speech you're writing:

- First, second, third. . .
- Rhetorical questions (e.g. So why should this be a problem? What does it really mean? Now why is that so important?)
- To illustrate the point. . .
- On the one hand. . .
- On the other hand. . .
- Looking at it from another perspective. . .
- For example. . .
- As I mentioned earlier. . .
- Let's take a closer look. . .
- But more important than that. . .
- Here's how it works in theory. . .
- Here's how it works in actual practice. . .
- Therefore. . .
- Here's a case in point. . .
- Let's begin with. . .
- Now let's turn to. . .
- According to. . .
- That's only one example. . .
- To summarize (To sum up, In closing). . .
- That's one issue (problem, solution, idea). . .
- Here's yet another issue (problem, solution, idea). . .
- However. . .
- Furthermore. . .
- That was yesterday. . .
- Here's where we're at today. . .

Use Humor
Where It Fits

The tests you applied to supporting material (is it relevant, accurate, recent, typical, sufficient, meaningful, appropriate, interesting, vivid?) can also be used to test whether humor should be used in the speech. Your observations in the initial meetings will tell you whether the speaker is comfortable with humor and what kind of humor works best. The general rule is to use humor only if it is meaningful and appropriate for the occasion, the audience and the topic. Don't tell jokes just to tell jokes. Period.

In fact, very little of the humor in speeches by executives is in the form of jokes. More often it takes the form of self put-downs, asides, brief personal observations, one-liners, and aphorisms. An advantage in using short items is that if they're not funny, the speaker can quickly move on as if nothing happened, and most of the audience won't know that the attempt at humor has failed. In any case, apply the old speechwriting rule with regard to the use of humor in speeches: "When in doubt, leave it out."

Here are examples from executive speeches where humor was used appropriately.

1 As I contemplate the implications of the topic and the professionalism of this audience, I am inclined to take the position of the husband who came home one evening having taken one glass too many. As his wife tried to remove his overcoat, he slid gently down the wall to the carpet and said, "I think in this instance I will dispense with the usual formal comments and simply take questions from the floor!" [69]

2 Unlike the westerners who are often easily frustrated and even infuriated by apparent contradictions and problems, the Chinese glory in them. The Chinese have a very common response when asked about the current international political or economic scene: "There is great disorder and struggle under heaven, the situation is excellent." [70]

3 I'm honored to have been invited to be your guest here today. North Carolina State University has an outstanding record of academic excellence. And that's not just something I've heard. That's something I know first-hand—as we have 42 North Carolina State graduates doing a first-rate job for us at Ford.

I'd also like to take this opportunity to applaud the efforts of this university in taking a leadership role, in focusing attention on what must be the burning issue of the day for all

Americans: the future competitiveness of our country.

It's no surprise to any of you that competitiveness is a matter of broad discussion, even debate, just about everywhere these days—in universities and offices, on the factory floor and on the campaign trail—wherever people meet to talk about the issues. It's been the subject of newspapers, white papers, books, articles, symposia. In fact, in some circles today it's been rather irreverently referred to as the "C" word. And now I understand it's met the ultimate test—it's fair game in comic strips and comedy routines. One humorist said that competitiveness is a lot like "love." Everybody says it, everybody talks about it, but nobody really knows what it means.

But, at Ford, we do believe we've been learning the hard way what competitiveness means. And it means more than building a product and pricing it right. It encompasses product appeal and quality; costs and profits; and education, training and retraining of people; the use of technology; entrepreneurship; the relationships among trading nations, and the role of government in fostering a competitive environment.[71]

4 It is a great pleasure and privilege for me to address you here today. I've heard a lot about this class—and I have to admit that most of it was good. I know for a fact that you've learned to live with a lot of change in your personal lives. For eleven weeks you've been separated from your homes and your families. You've gone from familiar duties on the job to the unfamiliar ones at this academy. You've endured snoring roommates, lack of

privacy, and even the impromptu wild French can-can dances of Monsieur Jean Malpel. These are the times that try men's souls, indeed.

But your performance shows how well you've been able to adapt. You've all come away with college credits from the University of Virginia. And you've all come away physically fit. Many of you elected to meet the "challenge" of 20 extra hours of physical training on your free time. Together, you've lost a total of 388 pounds, and you've lost 10 feet and 3 inches from around your collective waists. To paraphrase the noted critic, Cyril Connolly, I can see that imprisoned in every fat National Academy class is a thin one wildly signaling to be let out.

But I know you're leaving with more than sound bodies and sound minds. I know you've learned one of the most important facts of life in today's world: that you must learn to live with and plan for change in your professional world.[72]

5 Now, I'm well aware that for a Canadian to speak outside of Canada, even briefly, on the subject of "Canada's problems," is a course fraught with risks. First, there's a risk (with any other audience) that knowledge of my country may not be more than "skin-deep." As Marilyn Monroe once said: "When you said Canada, I thought it would be up in the mountains somewhere."

Or, one might expect the alarming sort of compliment such as the young Disraeli gave us, when he remarked: "I am not one of those who believe that the destiny of Canada must inevitably be annexation with the United States. Canada possesses all the elements of a great independent country. It is destined, I sometimes say to myself, to become the Russia of the New World."

Then, there is always the cynic's response. As John Robert Colombo put it: "Canada could have enjoyed English government, French culture, and American know-how. Instead, it ended up with English know-how, American culture and French government."

Much more often, though, any Canadian complaint of "hardship" simply falls on deaf ears. In my experience, the standard reply goes: "You Canadians are so fortunate. Let me tell you what WE have to contend with here!" [73]

6 All of this talk about a revolution in the information business doesn't frighten me, because I've known nothing but revolutionary new developments from the beginning. I feel like the man who was charged with drunkenness and, more seriously, with setting his bed on fire and damaging a building. The man pled guilty to being drunk; but he insisted he was innocent to the charge of setting his bed on fire. "The bed," he said, "was on fire when I got in it." [74]

7 If they sense a lack of consensus, the members of Congress are cautious to a fault. It was caution foremost in the mind of Senator Oliver Johnston of South Carolina many years ago when he gave this warning to his administrative aide.

Johnston, who was coming up for re-election, was troubled by his lack of anything substantial to write about in his Congressional newsletter to his constituents.

Finally he said to his assistant, "Why don't we write something against Communism?"

His aide agreed and came back with a crackerjack column exposing the evils of "godless atheistic Communism," putting the good senator four-square for Americanism.

Johnston read the prepared draft and nodded his approval.

As the aide went out the door, the senator called him back with this thought: "Wait a second. How many Communists do you think we have in South Carolina?"

"About five or six," said the aide.

"Well," said the senator, "You make mighty sure that this piece don't get sent to any of them! Ya hear!" [75]

8 Like the boss says to his secretary in a *Forbes* cartoon: "What a marvelous fiscal year—mergers, acquisitions, divestitures, deregulation, restructuring, maximized shareholder values! Refresh my memory—what business are we in?" [76]

9 It all comes down to a change in perspective—taking a different point of view.

At the turn of the century, a statue of General William Tecumseh Sherman was erected at the south front of the Treasury, where Pennsylvania Avenue bends an elbow to get around the building.

To the North, Sherman was a valiant hero. To the South, even at that time, he remained a symbol of the defeat and degradation suffered by the Confederacy, and he was hated by all true Southerners as the man who had devastated Georgia from Atlanta to the sea.

Secretary of the Treasury Lyman J. Gage was sensitive to this fact, and looked forward to presiding at the unveiling of the monument to Sherman on horseback with mixed emotions.

Finally, the day of the unveiling came—and the event passed without incident.

After it was over, he approached a southern newspaper correspondent and timidly asked what he thought of the monument.

"Well, Mr. Secretary," the reporter said, "from the north side where we stand, you see General Sherman as a soldier and gentleman astride his mighty charger—but from the south side all you can see is what we have always seen: a horse's rear end. . . ." [77]

10 In this competitive environment bankers must at times feel a little bit like Daniel Boone, who, when he was once asked whether he was ever lost in the woods, replied, "No, I can't say I was ever lost, but I was once bewildered." Directors who have traveled through the same bewildering terrain before can be the best guides to lead bankers on their journey through that territory. [78]

Colorful Characters

The mere mention of some names (W. C. Fields, Yogi Berra, and Charlie Brown) can build goodwill in many audiences. Following are a few quotations from colorful, quotable characters that were used in speeches by executives:

Attributed to Yogi Berra:

"I don't mind being surprised, so long as I know about it beforehand." [79]

"If people don't want to come to the ballpark, nobody's going to stop 'em." [80]

"It's *deja vu* all over again." [81]

"You can observe a lot by watching." [82]

Yogi Berra might have said, "The trouble with myths is that somebody might believe them." [83]

"Anybody who goes to see a psychiatrist should have his head examined." [84]

Attributed to W. C. Fields:

W. C. Fields said there were only three things he needed for a truly happy life: The love of a good woman, the respect of friends, and an incredible amount of money. He figured if he had the third, the first two were sure to follow. For W. C. Fields and business and industry, capital is important. . . .[85]

Many conglomerates are practicing corporate weight control by dumping yesterday's unfulfilled promises: products, services, acquisitions unrelated either to market unity or their core business, many left over from the not-so-long-ago days when conventional wisdom told us not to put all our eggs in one pocket. I think it was W. C. Fields who said: "If at first you don't succeed, then quit—there's no sense making a fool of yourself."[86]

Attributed to Charlie Brown:

One of America's best-known philosophers—Charlie Brown of the comic strip "Peanuts"—once said—"There is no problem so big—no challenge so awesome—no dilemma so frustrating or complicated—that one cannot simply walk away from it."[87]

The situation reminds me of a "Peanuts" cartoon I was told about recently. Lucy was using metaphor to explain life to Charlie Brown: "Charlie, on the great oceans are large ships that carry many passengers. On each ship there is a sundeck, and on that sundeck the passengers arrange their deck chairs. Some place them facing forwards so they can see where they are going. Some place them facing backwards so they can see where they have been. Now Charlie, on the great ship of life, which way will you face your deck chair, forwards or backwards?"

To which Charlie replied: "I can't even get mine unfolded." [88]

STEP 4
Review Draft with Speaker

It's now time to review the draft of the speech with the speaker. Until now the speaker has just seen the outline or parts of the speech. It's also time to suggest another important step in the process: do nothing for a while. Set the speech aside. It's hard to be objective about something you're in the process of creating. You will not be the same person in the same frame of mind tomorrow. It will surprise you how the errors or embarrassing shortcomings will leap out at you where the day before they were not visible. So wait a few days before you schedule your draft review meeting to give yourself an opportunity to take a fresh look at the material you've prepared.

Use a tape recorder at this session just like you did when you planned the outline with the speaker. Have the speaker read the draft—out loud—to change words and, if required, some sentence structures to better fit the speaker's style. The speaker has to adapt words and word combinations to a personal style of speaking. Perhaps the speaker may even strike out a paragraph or two. The speaker may also want to use some different supporting material in a spot or two or want to rework the introduction or whatever. That's good. That's healthy and the way it should be. Always remember, it is the speaker's speech. And the speaker has to be comfortable with it.

Make sure you have your research material with you so you can readily and easily offer various alternatives to the speaker, especially in the area of supporting material. For example, you may have used an analogy to support a particular point; but the speaker suggests that a detailed example would probably work better in that spot.

However, should the speaker start to tamper with the specific purpose or thesis or main points at this time, you're facing the possibility of a new speech. But that's unlikely to happen if you planned well—that is, set the course with the speaker in the planning stage and confirmed it later in the process. Of course, there are times when a compelling reason calls for making substantive changes in a speech. But those instances are rare.

Your comfort level should be reasonably high when you leave the speaker's office. That's because all you have to do now is make minor changes in the review draft and get it back to the speaker in final form. Your difficult task is finished. Now it's up to the speaker to rehearse, rehearse, rehearse.

Summary of the Speechwriting Process

This book has offered you step-by-step procedures to follow in writing a speech. They should keep you on target for writing a successful one. Eventually, after you've written a few speeches, you will probably work on more than one step at a time.

To summarize briefly:

- Analyze the audience and occasion.
- Meet with the speaker to discuss the topic and develop an outline of the speech body to include a specific purpose, thesis, two to five main points, and subpoints.
- Do research for a variety of supporting material.
- Meet again with the speaker to reconfirm the speech purpose, thesis and outline of the body, and to discuss supporting material you have identified.

- Write the body of the speech.
- Write the introduction.
- Write the conclusion.
- Test the supporting material.
- Check any humor in the speech draft for appropriateness.
- Make sure the introduction meets the criteria for a proper opening.
- Make sure the conclusion meets the criteria for a proper ending.
- Make sure the entire speech is written for the ear—that a good oral style has been used.
- Check language to make sure that it is clear, vivid and appropriate.
- Make sure there are smooth transitions from point to point.
- Rewrite the speech draft.
- Review the speech draft with the speaker to make non-substantive final changes that better fit the speaker's style.
- Write the final draft of the speech.

ENDNOTES

The number in parenthesis after an entry in this section is the retrieval number of the speech from *The Executive Speaker®* Company's extensive library of executive speeches. The full text of any of the speeches quoted in this book can be ordered for a nominal fee by calling 513-294-8493' or writing to *The Executive Speaker®*, Box 292437, Dayton, Ohio 45429.

1. James E. Lukaszewski, *Executive Action*, April 1989.

2. Jerry Tarver, University of Richmond, "Communication and Credibility: Corporate Speechmaking in an Incredulous Age," delivered at International Association of Business Communicators, Chicago, March 11, 1981. (312)

3. John R. Bonée, Illinois Bell, "The Care and Feeding of the Executive Speaker: A Few Age Old Principles of Effective Oratory," delivered at National Conference of Public Relations Students Society of America, Chicago, November 9, 1981. (507)

4. Allen Born, AMAX, Inc., "800 Days: Trauma, Decision, Action," delivered at Harvard University Business School alumni luncheon, Greenwich, September 21, 1987. (2470)

5. Milton Dickens, *Speech: Dynamic Communication*, 2nd ed. (New York City: Harcourt, Brace & World, Inc., 1963), p. 132.

6. Jane Blankenship, *Public Speaking: A Rhetorical Perspective*, 2nd ed. (Englewood Cliffs, New Jersey: Prentice-Hall, 1972), p. 156.

7. Philip Lesly, The Philip Lesly Co., "Effective Communication," delivered at Canadian Public Relations Society, Winnipeg, June 23, 1982. (609)

8. F. Gregory Fitz-Gerald, American Express Co., "Capital for Business: It Seeks Excellence Too," delivered at Seattle Rotary Club, August 22, 1984. (1300)

9. Harold J. Corbett, Monsanto Co., "The Best of the Thieves: Restoring Trust in Business," delivered at Oklahoma Jaycees, Stillwater, February 16, 1985. (1368)

10. C. M. Kittrell, Phillips Petroleum Co., "There's No Such Thing as a Free Press," delivered at Association of Educators in Journalism, University of Florida, Gainesville, August 8, 1984. (1233)

11. Lois DeBakey, Baylor College of Medicine, "Our National Priority: Education or Entertainment?," delivered at Houston Writing Project benefit luncheon, Houston, February 27, 1987. (2388)

12. Kenneth W. Cannestra, Lockheed Aeronautical Systems Company, "Quality: America's Greatest Challenge," delivered at the American Production and Inventory Control Society, New Orleans, February 27, 1989. (3095)

13. Paul. F. Oreffice, Dow Chemical Co., "Courting Disaster: Our Lawsuit Crisis," delivered at Shavano Institute, Scottsdale, Arizona, January 26, 1987. (2466)

14. George V. Grune, Reader's Digest Association, Inc., "The Pitfalls and Potential of International Marketing," delivered at Babcock Graduate School of Business, Wake Forest University, Winston-Salem, North Carolina, September 27, 1985. (1744)

15. A. W. Dahlberg, Southern Company Services, Inc., "Never Forget the First Law of Wingwalking," delivered at Public Utilities Conference, Atlanta, September 1, 1987. (2448)

16. Louis V. Tomasetti, General Electric Co., "Facing Reality in the Nuclear Industry," delivered at Atomic Industrial Forum, Washington, D.C., November 12, 1984. (1326)

17. Edward Bleckner, Jr., Racal-Milgo, "1987 Industry Outlook for Data Communications," delivered at American Electronics Association-Florida Council, Orlando, March 4, 1987. (2252)

18. Richard E. Wilkes, North American Mortgage Co., "Mortgage Megatrends," delivered at Austin Association of Professional Mortgage Women, Austin, September 15, 1987. (2456)

19. Rowland C. Frazee, Royal Bank of Canada, "Technology Today and Tomorrow: The Business View," delivered at CANJAC Business and Youth Conference (Junior Achievement), Edmonton, Alberta, August 21, 1984. (1237)

20. Sydney Gruson, The New York Times Co., remarks on the outlook for newspapers, delivered at Institute of Newspaper Controllers and Finance Officers, Dearborn, Michigan, undated. (719)

21. T. Mitchell Ford, Emhart Corp., "Communications: Achilles' Heal or Secret Weapon?" delivered at International Human Resources Conference, Enfield, Connecticut, September 19, 1985. (1553)

22. David S. Tappan, Jr., Fluor Corp., "The Chinese Mean Business--And It Isn't Business as Usual," delivered at Institutional Investor Magazine CEO Roundtable, Palm Beach, Florida, January 11, 1985. (1347)

23. Willard C. Butcher, Chase Manhattan Corp., commencement remarks, delivered at A. B. Freeman School of Business, Tulane University, New Orleans, May 15, 1987. (2459)

24. Dr. Joseph F. Boyle, American Medical Association, remarks on responsibilities and challenges in health care, delivered at Town Hall of California, San Francisco, March 20, 1985. (1476)

25. Don Bates, The Bates Co., Inc., "New Technology and Public Relations: The Reality, the Challenges, the Future," delivered at Annual Conference of Virginia Public Relations Society, Virginia Beach, Virginia, May 12, 1987. (2428)

26. John Crutcher, U.S. Postal Rate Commission, remarks on the U.S. Postal Service, delivered at Annual Chapter Officers' Conference of the National Association of Postmasters of the United States, February 20, 1984. (1096)

27. Janice Shaw Crouse, Taylor University, "The Managerial Woman: Settling In, Branching Out, Moving Up," delivered at Career Women's Council, Marion, Indiana, August 19, 1986. (2176)

28. Donald C. Garrison, Tri-County Technical College, "Training and Retraining Americans," delivered at Trustees Association of Community Colleges, Spokane, May 16, 1986. (2178)

29. Stanley A. Marach, Stat-A-Matrix Institute, "The Control of Quality in the U.S.A.," delivered at Objectif Export Stategie Qualite, Lyon, France, June 10, 1987. (2437)

30. Wayne C. Anderson, Nabisco Brands, Inc., "Corporate Government Relations," delivered at The Wharton School, University of Pennsylvania, Philadelphia, October 31, 1984. (1344)

31. Robert L. Clarke, Office of the Comptroller of the Currency, remarks on the role of management in bank failures, delivered at Exchequer Club, Washington, D.C., January 20, 1988. (2591)

32. Thomas G. Labrecque, Chase Manhattan Corp., "A Radical Approach to Banking Reform: Legalize Competition," delivered at the University of Richmond Business School, Richmond, Virginia, February 12, 1987. (2310)

33. Bennett E. Bidwell, Chrysler Corp., "Trade and Competition: Where the Rubber Meets the Road," delivered at The Rubber Association of Canada, February 17, 1987. (2273)

34. Howard Goldfeder, Federated Department Stores, Inc., remarks on success in a competitive marketplace, delivered at Edison Electric Institute convention, Cincinnati, June 8, 1987. (2484)

35. C. J. Silas, Phillips Petroleum Company, "A Question of Scruples: Repairing Our Moral Compass," delivered at the Alabama Business Hall of Fame Dinner, Tuscaloosa, Alabama, March 6, 1989. (3104)

36. Donald R. Beall, Rockwell International Corp., remarks on the aerospace industry, ethics and technology, delivered at WESCON Electronic Show and Convention, Anaheim, California, November 17, 1986. (2386)

37. James A. Baker, General Electric Company, remarks on competition, manufacturing, technology, and engineers, delivered at Assembly Technology Conference, September 20, 1983. (972)

38. E. Grady Bogue, Louisiana State University, "A Friend of Mine: Notes on the Gift of Teaching," delivered at Memphis State University, May 7, 1988. (2846)

39. John J. Phelan, Jr., The New York Stock Exchange, remarks on the evolution of the New York Stock Exchange, delivered at the Executive Club of Chicago, October 15, 1982. (1073)

40. Malcolm T. Stamper, The Boeing Company, "If We Are Smart," delivered at the Annual National Educational Conference of the National Contract Management Association, Los Angeles, July 22, 1988. (2792)

41. Patricia A. Wier, Encyclopaedia Britannica Inc., "Our Faltering Educational System: How Technology Can Help," delivered at IBM Media Industry Executives Conference, Palm Springs, California, April 14, 1986. (1963)

42. Thomas R. Horton, American Management Association, "That Old Management Magic," delivered at Commonwealth Club of California, San Francisco, October 5, 1987. (2583)

43. Richard J. Ferris, UAL, Inc., remarks at annual shareholders meeting, New York City, April 24, 1986. (1849)

44. Monte Haymon, Packaging Corporation of America, "Manufacturers Need More Leaders Not Managers," delivered at Young Executives Club of Chicago, December 1986. (2209)

45. Sid Cato, Sid Cato Communications, Inc., "Writing Well for Investors," delivered at National Investor Relations Institute, New Jersey Chapter, Saddle Brook, New Jersey, November 13, 1986.

46. Robert E. Allen, American Telephone and Telegraph Company, "Commitments Sought Require Commitments Kept," delivered at the World Affairs Council, San Francisco, March 28, 1988. (2794)

47. See Allen Born, Note 4.

48. E. John P. Browne, Standard Oil Production Company (BP America), "Thriving on a Diet of Boom and Bust," delivered at the Forum Club of Houston, March 25, 1988. (2773)

49. Lloyd E. Reuss, General Motors Corp., remarks on change, reorganization and competition in the auto industry, delivered at Grand Rapids Chamber of Commerce, Grand Rapids, Michigan, January 28, 1987. (2368)

50. Walt Williams, General Electric Co., "Customer Service at GE: Miles to Go Before We Sleep," delivered at Customer Service Conference, Fairfield, Connecticut, February 25, 1987. (2290)

51. Robert D. Kilpatrick, Connecticut General Corporation, "Give Business a Chance," delivered at the Annual American Chamber of Commerce Executives Management Conference, Hartford, Connecticut, October 13, 1981. (414)

52. George W. Wilson, Concord Monitor (New Hampshire), "Challenges and New Technology Add Up to Remarkable Times in Newspaper Advertising," delivered at Association of Newspaper Classified Advertising Managers, San Diego, June 22, 1987. (2514)

53. Richard E. Heckert, E.I. du Pont de Nemours and Co., "The Crash of '87: A Timely Reminder to Balance the Books," delivered at Economic Club of Detroit, November 16, 1987. (2540)

54. Frank P. Doyle, General Electric Co., remarks on labor relations and change, delivered at International Brotherhood of Electrical Workers, Toronto, September 18, 1986. (2352)

55. Lloyd E. Reuss, General Motors Corp., "Leadership in Today's General Motors," delivered at General Motors Alumni Dinner Meeting, Southfield, Michigan, October 14, 1986. (2154)

56. John L. Clendenin, BellSouth Corp., "An Iceberg Down South," delivered at Southern Association of Colleges and Schools, New Orleans, December 9, 1987. (2769)

57. Donald J. Atwood, General Motors Corporation, remarks on change and competitiveness in the global economy, delivered at Indiana University-Kokomo, Kokomo, Indiana, November 5, 1987. (2725)

58. Joseph N. Hankin, Westchester Community College, "You Ain't Seen Nothin' Yet," delievered at Opening Dinner of the Freshman Year Experience Conference, University of South Carolina, Columbia, December 4, 1988. (3019)

59. Alfred S. Warren, Jr., General Motors Corporation, remarks on the freedom to be unreasonable, delivered at Michigan Freedom Foundation, Camp Grayling, Michigan, August 5, 1988. (2854)

60. Howard M. Love, National Steel Corporation, "Reindustrialization: Friend or Foe?" delivered at Economic Club of Detroit, November 17, 1980. (268)

61. Sandra Yates, Matilda Publications, remarks on women and political issues, delivered at New York State Fair, Syracuse, September 7, 1988. (2860)

62. Alexander A. Cunningham, General Motors Corporation, "Doing the Right Things Right," delivered at American Society of Body Engineers Annual Technical Seminar, Bloomfield Township, Michigan, October 11, 1984. (1277)

63. Fred G. Steingraber, A. T. Kearney, Inc., "U.S. Competitiveness," delivered at Society of Manufacturing Engineers' Autofact 1987, Detroit, November 10, 1987. (2711)

64. Peter Huber, Manhattan Institute, "Who Will Protect Us From Our Protectors?" delivered at Shavano Institute, Cleveland, November 16, 1987. (2681)

65. John W. Felton, McCormick & Company, Inc., "In A Word," delivered at awards luncheon of Public Relations Society of America, Washington, D.C., November 10, 1986. (2704)

66. Richard J. Ferris, UAL, Inc., "Deregulation: After the Sunset Comes the Dawn," delivered at Economic Club of Chicago, February 28, 1985. (1401)

67. L. A. Iacocca, Chrysler Corporation, "Remarks on the Statue of Liberty," delivered at Year of Liberty Gala Concert, Washington, D.C., October 28, 1985. (1632)

68. See John R. Bonée, Note 3.

69. Robert V. Lindsay, Morgan Guaranty Trust Company, "The International Monetary Scene in the 80s," delivered before the 11th World Congress of the International Association of Financial Executives Institutes, Sydney, Australia, October 27, 1980. (232)

70. Tod O. Clare, American Motors Corporation, "The Business Challenge in China: Separating the Yin from the Yang," delivered at Doing Business in China Conference, University of Wisconsin, Madison, September 4, 1986. (2156)

71. Donald E. Petersen, Ford Motor Company, "It's Our Move," delivered at Emerging Issues Forum, North Carolina State University, Raleigh, March 11, 1988. (2631)

72. William S. Sessions, Federal Bureau of Investigation, remarks on planning and training for change in law enforcement, delivered at 151st Session of the National Academy, Quantico, Virginia, December 18, 1987. (2595)

73. Allan R. Taylor, Royal Bank of Canada, "Canada Revisited," delivered at Canada Club, London, England, November 18, 1987. (2750)

74. Helen K. Copley, Copley Press, Inc., "The Wiring of America--The New Information Age," delivered at Los Angeles Rotary Club, May 7, 1982. (629)

75. Richard V. Fitzgerald, Office of the Comptroller of the Currency, remarks on banking, delivered at IFA Conference on Insurance, Chicago, June 10, 1987. (2395)

76. Richard J. Ferris, UAL, Inc., "World Aviation: Evolution of the Species," delivered at Atlanta Rotary Club, June 9, 1986. (1983)

77. Richard V. Fitzgerald, Office of the Comptroller of the Currency, "Banzai Banking—Sayonara Segmentation," delivered at Exchequer Club, Washington, D.C., November 19, 1986. (2177)

78. Robert L. Clarke, Office of the Comptroller of the Currency, "Beyond the Call of Duty," delivered at Kentucky Bankers Association, Louisville, September 8, 1986. (2039)

79. David Peterson, Premier of Ontario, remarks on the economic outlook for Ontario, delivered at Conference Board of Canada Outlook Conference, Toronto, October 3, 1985. (1989)

80. David Peterson, Premier of Ontario, remarks on the economic outlook for Ontario, delivered at Ontario Chamber of Commerce, Toronto, May 26, 1986. (1977)

81. Robert L. Clarke, Office of the Comptroller of the Currency, remarks on regulation of the financial services industry, delivered at Morin Center for Banking Law Studies, Boston, May 2, 1986. (1929)

82. Donald K. Grierson, General Electric Company, "Eyes on Automation," delivered at Kidder, Peabody & Co., Institutional Investment Seminar, New York City, May 9, 1984. (1173)

83. James J. Howard, Ameritech, "The Mythology of Telecommunications," delivered at Communications Daily Telecommunications Conference, Washington, D.C., June 11, 1984. (1210)

84. Donald E. Petersen, Ford Motor Company, "Yogi Berra Was Right," delivered at Economic Club of Detroit, November 4, 1985. (1635)

85. Robert J. Lanigan, Owens-Illinois, Inc., "Capital Formation in the Real World," delivered at University of Chicago, October 31, 1979. (78)

86. Alfred Powis, Noranda Mines Limited, remarks on achieving success in the 1980s, delivered at Toronto Junior Board of Trade/Toronto Jaycees, Toronto, February 16, 1982. (660)

87. Nicholas L. Reding, Monsanto Company, "Leading American Agriculture into the 21st Century," delivered at College of Agriculture, University of Missouri, Columbia, May 14, 1983. (879)

88. Rowland C. Frazee, Royal Bank of Canada, "Canadian Confidence: A Long Night's Journey into Day," delivered at 53rd Annual Meeting of the Canadian Chamber of Commerce, Ottawa, September 19, 1982. (684)

Index